A COOKBOOK FOR A KNUCKLEHEAD

Bachelor, New Graduate, Beginner, and other Spoiled Brats

Harold W. Pearman

Outskirts Press, Inc.
Denver, Colorado

The opinions expressed in this manuscript are solely the opinions of the author and do not represent the opinions or thoughts of the publisher. The author has represented and warranted full ownership and/or legal right to publish all the materials in this book.

A Cookbook for a Knucklehead
Bachelor, New Graduate, Beginner, and Other Spoiled Brats
All Rights Reserved.
Copyright © 2011 Harold W. Pearman
v 4.0

Cover Illustration by Bobbi Switzer.

Cover Illustration © 2011 Outskirts Press, Inc. All Rights Reserved. Used with permission.
This book may not be reproduced, transmitted, or stored in whole or in part by any means, including graphic, electronic, or mechanical without the express written consent of the publisher except in the case of brief quotations embodied in critical articles and reviews.

Outskirts Press, Inc.
http://www.outskirtspress.com

ISBN: 978-1-4327-5550-8

Library of Congress Control Number: 2010935419

Outskirts Press and the "OP" logo are trademarks belonging to Outskirts Press, Inc.

PRINTED IN THE UNITED STATES OF AMERICA

Presentation:

I am so happy to present this book to my favorite KNUCKLEHEAD, _____. I hope that you will finally learn how to cook, and hopefully not starve to death. May this book put a smile on your face, and some unbelievably good food in your tummy. With Love and my Respect;

_____

PS: The recipes are real and are absolutely delightful. Enjoy them all.

Dedicated to Jewell Dean Pearman, better known as Mom, for teaching me to cook by making it fun when I was young. You are a fabulous cook, a patient teacher, and a loving mother.

Introduction

Well, it has finally happened. I have published my cooking book, which I have been working on for over two years now. As you will see, and understand as you go through this publication (I just love saying and writing that word), there are a number of things that need to be explained in advance, which I will attempt to do in this Introduction.

First and foremost, it is imperative that you have a sense of humor. If you don't, the odds of you enjoying this book are somewhat remote. If you do have a good sense of humor, as the person who bought this book for you believed you do, then read on KNUCKLEHEAD.

As you now know, YOU, as the cook, are now known as KNUCKLEHEAD. This should be construed as a term of endearment, and not as a derogatory moniker of some sort. Whenever anyone takes on a difficult task, such as learning to really cook, a certain amount of failure is inevitable. Using my newly earned "author's license" I have chosen to use the term KNUCKLEHEAD, recalled from my childhood growing up in Mountain Grove, Missouri, to describe all of the new cooks reading this book. I can't remember any specifics of when this term was used to describe me, but certainly heard it enough to know how it must have applied. It stuck with me, and I remember the context under which it was intended; failure of some sort, that could have probably been prevented with a little fore thought. So it is with much affection and good-natured ribbing that I hereby bestow that moniker on you. Perhaps I should mention by the way, that a true KNUCKLEHEAD cannot touch all of their top teeth with their tongue. All KNUCKLEHEAD after reading that sentence will try it, feel superior momentarily, realize that sentence was a lie, and then smile. That was just too easy. All KNUCKLEHEADS will be smiling at this point, so it is with all the respect due that I say, "Welcome aboard KNUCKLEHEAD. This is going to be fun."

The recipes in this book are honest-to-goodness good recipes that I have learned and developed over the past several years. Many from my mother, some from friends, and some from relatives, but none of them from books. They represent comfort food with a taste of the Midwest and the memories and influence of my childhood, a smithering of accent from the Cajuns in New Orleans, a dab of the west, and a whole bunch of experimenting to come up with "Oh yeah; that tastes good." I have only one corroborator and advisor involved with this publication, that being my best friend Pennie. For her unwavering support and encouragement in life, I have allowed her, on each recipe page, to "Throw you a bone"; an old military term that I learned, which loosely translates to mean "helpful hint." You will find these helpful hints on the bottom left side of each recipe, and I highly advise you to both read and heed Pennie's hints.

I have intentionally chosen very simple recipes that utilize products and ingredients that may already exist in your kitchen and refrigerator, or can be easily and inexpensively procured at your local grocery. The recipes are also meant to be quite uncomplicated, to allow you to achieve the success of a great meal, while you learn the various cooking techniques required for future endeavors with more involved cook books. Perhaps now is a good time to point you in that direction, for reference later, by telling you that it is my opinion that Paula Dean and Bobby Flay are two of the best chefs in America. Any of their cooking books and products, you may count on to be high quality and/or superb food. However for now you are not quite ready for them. For that reason we will take the time to teach you a few basics necessary for any cooking endeavor, as well as several very simple every day dishes and side dishes that are not normally found in the more involved cook books. After you have prepared many of the recipes in this book, you will have learned most of the basic techniques needed to handle the more involved recipes, and gained enough confidence in your own skills, to take on any recipe you choose. Yes, even you KNUCKLEHEAD. It is my goal to make you use that sausage between your ears for something besides a hat rack.

At the top left corner of each recipe you will see a small balloon with various names or references. The names represent friends and family who helped with that recipe, notes on personal favorites, or in some cases just old friends I remember and wanted to recognize and say Hi to. This book has been a labor of love for me, and I hope you will indulge this bit of personal sentimentality from the author.

At the bottoms of each page you will find a few sentences of wisdom. Obviously since you are a **KNUCKLEHEAD** you are in dire need of wisdom, and I have kept track of many bits of wisdom over the years to share with you. Some are my own, some remembered, and I am sure many are borrowed or attributable to people wiser than both of us. It is not my intent to steal anyone else's work, but rather give tribute to their pearls of wisdom and simply share them. Therefore, in advance, if anyone believes these bits of literary genius to be their own, then accept my apology and my thanks for being able to share them with my **KNUCKLEHEAD** friends.

Please note that I have done all food preparation myself, have taken all of my own pictures, and written all of my own text. Unlike other cooking publications, I have chosen to show you pictures of the dishes in progress, as well as complete, and to use normal utensils and products found in ordinary homes, and not just in gourmet chef kitchens. The pictures are taken in my kitchen, using real pots and pans with some stains or discoloring, much as you will no doubt use. I did not hire a professional photographer (that little fact should become blatantly obvious to you as you go through the recipes) but instead snapped all photographs myself. My intent is for you to learn how to cook under real-life conditions, not marvel at or drool over the pictures. You will also see many product names in this book. I have received no compensation from any company, and if I show, specify, or use any one particular product, it is because I like it, it works, and tastes good.

Jim Valvano, ex-coach at North Carolina State before his death from cancer several years ago, was a man I followed and admired. In a parting speech before his death he stated, and I paraphrase, "No man could want more in a day than to laugh, cry, and hope and dream." So you **KNUCKLEHEAD** let's have a perfect day right now; pick out a recipe, cut up an onion, and dream of the wonderful food you are going to learn how to create. That should cover all three bases for Jimmy.

Bon Appétit..............

KNUCKLEHEAD.

TABLE OF CONTENTS

Basics	3-11
Breakfast	13-21
Salads	23-31
Entrée's	33-51
Side dishes	53-65
Desserts	67-75
Drinks	77-93

KNUCKLEHEAD NOTES:

Basics For a Knucklehead

Bachelor, New Graduate, Beginner, and other Knuckleheads

The basic premise of this cookbook, is that you are a novice in the kitchen. For that reason, I am including some very basic information on cooking and recipe preparation that you may or may not already know. Browse through these first pages, even if you do find them a bit tedious at first, as I am sure that you can pick up a few useful tips or tidbits of information of which you were not previously aware.

Please pay particular attention to the pages on temperature controls, timers, and safety. I know this is not the most interesting section in the book, but I am also sure that if you will read, and heed, my advice, you will save yourself some heartache, if not a little skin. Be careful, Knuckleheads, and when all else fails; think.

Pots/Pans/Utensils

Choose Wisely

Equipment

Large sauce pan with lid

Small sauce pan with lid

Large pot with handle and lid

Small pot with handle and lid

3-5 quart casserole (Dutch oven)

6 quart covered stockpot

Assortment of wood spoons

Assorted utensils of tongs, spatulas, large fork, large spoon, and ladle

I know that most of the equipment you have now is pass me down or an eclectic assortment at best. Go to a major department store and pick up the balance of what you need. It is very affordable and will pay for itself in the meals you save. You could adequately stock your entire kitchen with new equipment for less than $400. It will be worth it to you in the long run.

A Bone from Pennie

Remember as we get started, you KNUCKLEHEAD, that your significant other doesn't expect much from you, and I for one am sure you will not disappoint.

Non-stick (Teflon) cookware should only be used at low to medium heat, utilizing only soft or wooden utensils with its use.

Glass lids let you watch your food cook, and can help prevent overcooking or burning of the dish.

Aluminum and copper pots and pans heat very quickly and evenly. Cast iron, such as the Dutch oven shown, holds in heat best, and is great for slow cooking recipes. I recommend an enamel finish on the cast iron for cleaning purposes.

Not all pots or pans are oven safe. If you are unsure, research it on-line, and always keep an eye on them. Likewise not all pots and pans can go in a dishwasher, so be careful.

Directions

The exact size of your pots and pans is not too critical at this stage of your cooking career, but you do need some assortment. A suggested basic package, shown in picture **A**, from left to right, consists of a large and small pot, a large and small sauce pan, a cast iron Dutch oven or casserole, and a large stockpot. You may not have most or even all of these, but do the best you can and try and accumulate these pieces over time. You may want to pass by some garage or estate sales which almost always have some *previously loved* cooking items at ridiculously low prices.

Picture **B** shows you a fairly complete beginners package of utensils you will want to obtain. From left to right on the back row is a slotted turner, a flat turner, a large spoon, a slotted spoon, a slotted round-end wooden spoon, a ladle, and a pasta server. On the front row from left to right is a basting brush, a whisk, a spatula, a pizza cutter, tongs, a large/long fork, and a carrot peeler.

I wanted to show you the two basic types of lids in use today, which are shown in picture **C**. Notice they look the same at first glance, but the one on the left has a tiny vent hole in it. This vent hole allows steam to escape, rather than hold it inside like the other solid lid, which results in a faster loss of moisture. In some of the longer cooking-time recipes, it will be necessary to make sure and add water during the cooking process, if the contents are becoming too thick, or scorching, from water loss. You will lose some water with both types of lids, but much slower with a unvented and well fitting lid. None of the recipes in this book require the use of a vented lid.

A

B

C

Learn from other peoples mistakes; You won't enjoy making them all yourself.

4

Knives & Cutting

Careful

Equipment

Chef knife with 8 inch blade

Santoku knife with 5 inch blade

Serrated utility knife

Paring knife

Sharpening steel rasp

Grater box

Note: While researching this brief section, I found, at one point, over 82 specific different knives before I quit counting. Knives are a personal thing to serious chefs, and each person has his or her own likes and dislikes, based on type of tip, balance, length and flexibility, as well as curvature and edge type. Find a knife with a grip that is comfortable and not slick, and learn to master that blade. Each type of knife has a task for which it is designed and best suited for it's use.

A Bone from Pennie

You don't have to pay attention here KNUCKLEHEAD. You can be just like my friends Knuckles Cobb, Lefty Ballay, and Stumpy Still. They didn't listen either. You will lose some water with both types of lids, but much slower with a unvented and well fitting lid. Otherwise learn and use these cutting techniques.

The chef knife is large and long and can be difficult to properly manage by beginner chefs. The Santoku knife looks a little odd but the thicker blade where the bolster attaches to the handle protects your cutting hand fingers from sliding forward onto the blade and cutting yourself. I suggest you get one of these to get started.

A sharp blade is tantamount to being able to properly prepare your foods. Technique is just as important to get the food properly prepared, and most important to your safety. Learn from the start to curl your holding hand fingers inward away from the blade, which prevents them from being trapped under the blade, and sliced

Directions

Picture **A** shows the six basic cutting devices you will want to have, and become acquainted with, for use with this book, as well as day to day use. From left to right is an 8-inch Chef knife, a 5-inch Santoku knife, a 5-inch serrated utility knife, a small paring knife, a round sharpening steel rasp, and a simple grating box with handle.

The Chef knife is very versatile and commonly used for slicing and dicing vegetables such as onions, potatoes, squash, etc. and firm fruits such as apples and pears.

The Santoku knife is used for much the same purpose as the chef knife, but has the kullen ripples on the edge to help prevent the food sticking to the knife. This knife has become my favorite and I use it for most of my cutting.

Use the serrated knife for bread and soft veggies or fruits. A paring knife is used to peel apples, potatoes, oranges, etc.

When sharpening your knife blades, place the tip of the sharpening steel rasp on a cutting board. Place the bottom of the blade, nearest the knife handle, on the rasp at a small angle. Using a modest amount of pressure, bring the blade across the rasp maintaining the slight angle. Repeat motion for the other side of the knife blade, and continue to repeat this alternating routine 6 to 8 times. Do not use on serrated knife. <u>**ALWAYS**</u> move the blade away from your hand and body!

You cannot survive without a cutting board. Picture **B** shows a cheap plastic one that I use. Whenever I run the dishwasher, I am able to throw this plastic one in for sanitization, whereas a wooden cutting board cannot go in the dishwasher. I do not recommend cutting meat on a wooden board, as it will tend to hold and absorb bacteria.

The grater shown in picture **C** is used to grate potatoes, cheeses, fruits, and vegetables. Shown here is the grater I used to slice a potato to use in hash browns. Off to the side you see a stack of onion bits already prepared with the grater. This device is extremely sharp, and possibly more likely than the knives above to draw blood. Always push down and away from yourself, and <u>**DO NOT**</u> allow your finger tips to graze the cutting holes. Throw away that last little chunk of potato or apple, or eat it, but don't try and get that last little sliver.

A

B

C

When you get depressed or just feeling sorry for yourself, stop counting your troubles and count your blessings.

Measuring

No "oops" please

Equipment

1 set of small measuring spoons

1 set of large measuring spoons

1 measuring cup

Note 1: There are three measurements/quantities that you need to put to memory:

The correct amount- The amount or measurement I tell you to use in a recipe.

Too much- An amount more than I tell you to use in a recipe.

Too little- Less than I tell you to use in a recipe.

Note 2:

TBSP = 1 Tablespoon = 1/2 ounce

TSP = 1 Teaspoon = 1/3 Tablespoon

4 TBSP = 1/4 cup

1 cup = 8 fluid ounces

A Bone from Pennie

Maybe you better start breaking those pills in half KNUCKLeHead. I am starting to see some disturbing patterns with your measurements.

When using either the small measuring spoons or the large measuring cups to measure dry ingredients, be sure and use a straight edge such as a butter knife to scrape away the excess ingredients mounded in the spoons or cups. Each measurement device should be full and level with the top rim.

More experienced cooks will simply guess at many of these quantities, and from years of practice can generally get it right. However until you learn many of the basics in this book, I highly recommend that you measure each quantity in accordance with the prescribed amount in the recipe. Many ingredients such as baking soda are very volume sensitive, and some spices such as cloves for example can be overpowering if not used in the correct quantity.

Directions

You will need three basic types of measuring devices. When measuring larger quantities of liquid ingredients such as milk, oil, and water, a liquid measuring cup, seen in picture **A**, is most often used. The one shown on the right is specifically referred to as an angled measuring cup, and the one on the left is a standard measuring cup. Either one is suitable. I strongly prefer the angled measuring cup as it allows me to pour ingredients into the cup and read the volume quantities on the inside of the cup, without picking it up. With the standard cup you have to either bend over and look at the side of the cup, or hold it up to eye level to check the quantity within. The second of those options can lead to spills when using full measurements.

Picture **B** contains large measuring cups. You can use these for either dry or liquid ingredients, but most commonly these are used for the dry ingredients. Shown from left to right is a 1 cup, a 1/2 cup, a 1/3 cup, and a 1/4 cup measuring cup. These cups would normally be used with such items as flour and sugar. The measurement cups should be rinsed and cleaned before using them a second time in the same recipe.

The small measuring spoons shown here in picture **C**, from left to right, are 1 tablespoon, 1/2 tablespoon, 1 teaspoon, 1/2 teaspoon, and 1/4 teaspoon. These small spoons can be used for small quantities of either liquid or dry ingredients such as vanilla, spices, baking soda, etc. Be sure to rinse and dry each one after use as you may need the same spoon for other ingredients in the same recipe. For this reason, many cooks will have two sets of these; one for liquid and one for dry ingredients, to help speed up the food preparation, and not have to clean up during the process. Not shown is a "pinch" which I am hoping you can figure out.

Double-check your recipe and your measurement quantity, before you actually add them to your dish.

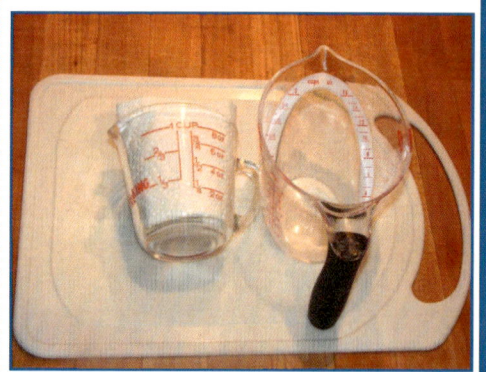

Never argue with an idiot. They will drag you down to their level and then beat you with experience.

Seasoning & Oils

Ahchoo!

Ingredients

Assorted seasonings

Olive oil

Vegetable oil

A Bone from Pennie

It appears ,KNUCKLeHead, that when you were born, the doctor missed your butt and smacked your head instead. Pay attention here.

Dry seasonings that are sprinkled, coat the outside surface of meats or vegetables and other ingredients. Only liquid seasonings penetrate meats or other products.

Perhaps the best advice for you when seasoning a dish is that less is better than more. You can add more seasoning later, but you cannot take seasoning off or out of a dish easily if at all. So until you learn which seasonings you like and wish to cook with, use a light hand and experiment with quantities, until you discover the desired level of seasoning that you prefer.

Most cooks today use ground pepper mills in lieu of the old standard black pepper. Ground peppercorns are one of my favorites, and commonly sold in small grinding mill bottles.

Directions

Picture **A** shows an assortment of seasonings. Of course salt and pepper are your basic must, shown at the top. I also wanted to show you a few special additives. On the left is my favorite brand of dry spice rub, used to season ribs and other meats. I find that if I lightly coat the meat with olive oil, and then literally rub the spice into the meat, that the spices stick better and remain on the meat after cooking. Then a garlic salt, a "coarse sea salt", which adds some texture to a dish and is absolutely perfect on my baked potato recipe, a garlic and herb seasoning, a general all-purpose seasoning which is very good with vegetables, and a Luzianne Cajun seasoning which is a little hotter than the others

Olive oil, shown in picture **B** is perhaps the most versatile of the variety of cooking oils on the market. I use it to coat meats and to cook meats in skillets, as well as some of the salad recipes. I am not a connoisseur of olive oils and cannot tell much difference in the standard varieties found in the grocery stores. For that reason, and due to the higher cost than standard cooking oils, I suggest that you choose one of the cheaper selections such as the store brand. There is also a large selection of olive oils today that are bottled and have ingredients added to them such as basil or peppers, etc., but these should not be used in the normal recipes, unless specified. *Olive oil with garlic* is shown.

Picture **C** shows a basic vegetable oil. I use corn oil, as shown, simply because I prefer it's taste to other oils. Most shoppers choose their oil of choice today, based on content of trans fats, cholesterol, calories, sodium, carbohydrates, etc. They all cook somewhat the same, at least in my opinion, so feel free to use vegetable oil, canola oil, corn oil, etc. somewhat interchangeably. Be careful with peanut oil. Some people are allergic to peanut products, and peanut oil does have a very different taste, and will noticeably alter the taste of your dish.

A

B

C

You can't listen while you are talking.

7

Timers & Safety

Are you listening

Equipment

Oven timer

Portable timer

Fire extinguisher

Pot holders

(Optional): Directions to nearest hospital or emergency care facility, the phone number of the fire station, and a big stick to beat the KNUCKLEHEAD that does not pay attention to these simple but critical instructions.

A Bone from Pennie

Those ears stuck on the side of your head KNUCKLEHEAD, are not just for decoration or to hang your glasses on. Set the timer and listen for it!

There probably is not a cook alive that has not at sometime grabbed a hot pot or pan and burned their hands and fingers. Invest in some good pot holders, whether a simple square padded one, or the oven mitten type that covers you entire hand. When removing something from the oven use two hands and protect each with some type of pot holder. The FBI is probably going to need your fingerprints one day, and I want you to have some to give them.

Very few dishes require high heat, so when setting your stove burner temperature, use some moderation and be careful of cooking above medium to medium high settings.

Handles and knobs get hot, depending on type of apparatus used.

Directions

Picture **A** shows the timer button on my personal oven, which is somewhat typical of the newer touch button oven models. Picture **B** is a typical type of cabinet-top portable timer. One of these types of timers is absolutely imperative for your personal safety as well as the well being of your home and belongings. Picture **C** is a small home and kitchen fire extinguisher available in most hardware or home & garden stores. If you blow off my suggestion of one of the timers, you KNUCKLEHEAD, then be sure you have the fire extinguisher.

Safety tips:

Always use a timer. It will save you many a burnt meal, for sure a pot or pan here and there, and just maybe your life or home.

Never let a pot boil dry, and never set an empty pot or pan back on a hot or lit burner. Always use an oven mitt or pot holder to handle hot pans or dishes, similar to the ones shown in picture **B**; pot holder on right and hand covering mitt on the left.

Your stove has different size burners for a reason. Select the burner that best suits the size of the pot or pan you are using, and never let the flames of a gas stove travel up the outside of your cooking utensil.

I suggest that you never leave a cooking item on a stove top, unattended. If hot oil or grease is involved then absolutely do not leave it unattended. A grease fire is difficult to put out, and has burned down many buildings and homes.

Keep children and pets away from a cooking area in general. No one ever plans on spilling or splashing hot liquids, but it happens every day.

Never put plastic handled pans in the oven.

Never allow a non-stick pot or pan to be used directly under the oven broiler.

Be careful and think at all times.

A

B

C

There is no greater challenge than to have someone relying upon you; and no greater satisfaction than to vindicate their expectation.

Ovens & Stove

Follow Directions

Equipment

1 oven

1 stove or stove top

1 microwave oven

1 timer (this is repetitive but is absolutely critical, and so I mention it to you again in this section).

Have I mentioned to you lately about always using a timer?

A Bone from Pennie

Where there is smoke there is fire, and very often a KNUCKLeHead. Learn to keep the heat and fire low while you still have eyebrows.

I don't have much extra advice to offer here, except to remind you to use a timer. Foods cooked at or above medium on the stove can run low or out of liquid very quickly and ruin the dish or the pot, or cause a fire, and so they demand constant monitoring. Foods cooked in the oven should always have a timer set, most importantly when using a broiler which can turn a piece of buttered French bread into a deadly frisbee quicker than you can say KNUCKLeHead three times.

When re-heating meats, try and use the oven if possible, as a microwave has a tendency to cause most meats to become rubbery, dry, or hard when re-heated.

Do not "over-defrost" in the microwave as it will *break-down* meats and adversely affect taste.

Directions

My oven, shown here in picture **A**, uses touch sensitive buttons in lieu of dials common on some older models. Take time to read the owners manual and learn what each of the oven settings is intended to be used for, and learn how to utilize the full potential of this piece of equipment. Ovens are most commonly used for baking, and recipes will often require baking times of 30 minutes up to 2 or 3 hours or longer. Always follow the directions of the recipe for cooking time. The broiler is located in the top of your oven. When baking, set your dishes in the middle or lower part of the oven, and when broiling set the dish in the upper section unless directed otherwise. A time of 5 to 10 minutes of broiling is a lot. Set your timer when broiling, or put the fire department on speed dial.

A typical gas burning stove top with six burners is shown in picture **B**. Notice the three different size burners to provide evenly distributed flames to the bottom of different size pots and pans. Most stoves use dials for the burner temperatures, with settings of low, medium, and high, and sometimes settings in between or a very low setting for simmer. Different stoves vary on the exact amount of heat at these settings, so when learning your recipes as well as the intricacies of your own particular stove, choose a lower setting when in doubt. Gradually increase temperatures over time until you achieve the desired temperature and or result. I have intentionally left the protective aluminum foil down, to show how to protect your appliance from burnt stains, that are difficult or impossible to remove. Simply remove the iron grates, and cut and fold aluminum foil around the burners, being sure not to cover the flame ports or the igniting striker. Reinstall the grates, and change out the foil every month or so as needed.

A microwave oven, shown here in picture **C** is a common fixture in most modern kitchens today. I cannot emphasize enough how important it is for you to read the owners manual on the microwave you use. There are so many pre-settings that are accurate and safe, and will allow you to do more with this piece of equipment than you thought possible. For repetitive items that you warm or cook in the microwave, make a small note of the settings and cooking time, and tape the note to the door for quick and easy reference. When defrosting it is much better to go short on the time, rather than long. You can always put the item back in for additional defrosting time.

A

B

C

You may fight and win many a good fight, but remember that for every warrior comes the day when his strength will fail him.

9

Boiling Foods

Hot, hot, hot

Ingredients

Water

Bag of rice

Box of pasta

Eggs

Note: Use any pot with handles and a lid, paying attention to selection of size as explained in the directions and hints.

A Bone from Pennie

If you are anywhere close to hunting season for KNUCKLEHEADS, then you better hide or at least practice ducking. Boiling water burns and scars whatever flesh it touches; immediately. Please use care and follow directions.

Off to the side of the boiled eggs is a burgundy colored egg slicer. This is a great inexpensive little kitchen tool that will help you with the appearance of your salads or dishes, and quite honestly I just find it fun to use.

Commonly used white rice is usually long grained rice. My personal favorite is a long grained *jasmine* rice which is used in most Japanese and Chinese restaurants. It is a little stickier in consistency but give it a try and see if you enjoy it.

The old adage of throwing a piece of pasta against the wall and if it sticks the pasta is done, is unreliable. Just follow the recipes KNUCKLEHEAD.

Directions

Rather than lecture you on the simple task of boiling water, I have elected to give you three of the most common boiled food recipes used in this book and most others. The first task in any boiling recipe is to select the proper pot or pan. Use a container that does not let the required amount of water rise above the halfway point on the side when all ingredients are in place.

Boiled eggs, shown in picture **A**, are a staple ingredient in many salads and other dishes. Place the number of eggs you wish to boil in the bottom of a pot (do not layer), fill the pot above top of eggs but no higher than halfway point of pot side, and bring to a boil on medium high heat. When water gets to a "rolling boil" continue boiling for 2 minutes, then turn heat off, cover with lid and let sit on the unlit burner for 20 to 30 minutes. Strain, crack, and peel.

Rice is so common in many recipes, and substitutes for potatoes in many gravy covered dishes today. Picture **B** shows a completed batch of rice in a large cooking pot with handle. Select the type of rice you like, whether white, brown, wild, etc. and **exactly** follow the cooking instructions on the bag or box. When complete, remove from heat, and serve while fresh and warm.

There are so many different types of pasta, I literally get confused when I go shopping to pick some up. Just like the rice recipe above, **exactly** follow the cooking instructions on the bag or box of the specific type of pasta you choose. Each different type of pasta cooks just a little bit differently, and for different lengths of time. Picture **C** shows a colander placed in the bottom of a sink, and the cooked pasta poured into the colander to drain. If desired you may run water over the pasta while it is in the colander in the sink, to rinse, or you can serve it immediately while it is still hot. Rinse with cold water if pasta is for a salad, and rinse with warm or hot water if pasta is for hot entrée.

A

B

C

Fear is just a limitation set by your imagination. Have courage.

> Gasconade gigging

Frying Foods

Ingredients & Equipment

1 bottle of oil

1 electric deep fat fryer

1 frying pan (sauce pan)

A Bone from Pennie

FYI there KNUCKLeHead, most people will eat animal droppings or old shoes if you fry them with butter or fresh oil. Don't be afraid to fry foods, just be careful.

When deep frying, make sure you let the oil get up to final temperature before you place ingredients into the oil. Carefully place (do not carelessly drop) your food to be fried into the hot oil, as the oil will splash and splatter.

When pan frying foods, it is recommended that you cover the pan with a lid. The lid will keep hot oil splatter in the pan, and will assist in keeping heat in the food being fried. Thick cuts of meat such as chicken and pork chops are sometimes difficult to get fully cooked on the inside without blackening the outside or drying out the meat. The lid helps.

Pan frying is a great way to prepare fish, using a similar method to the chicken dish above, but using corn meal and seasoning instead.

Directions

To fry a food, in simplistic terms, simply means to cook it in oil. There are two basic ways to accomplish this task. The first is the most common, and generally referred to as *deep frying*. As the name implies a pot or fryer vat is filled with oil and the food to be fried is fully emerged in the oil and not removed until it is fully cooked. Fast-food battered chicken as well as French fries are usually cooked in this manner. In picture **A** you can view some French fries being removed from an electric deep fat fryer. I actually do not recommend this type of frying for three very good reasons; the process is very dangerous with the large quantity of hot grease, it is extremely messy and difficult to clean up, and it is usually cheaper and easier to get this type of dish at a restaurant or fast food venue.

An easier and less messy way of frying foods, is referred to commonly as *pan fried*. By simply placing about 1/4 inch of the type of oil you prefer in the bottom of a flat skillet, then covering with a lid, you can fry your foods with less mess to clean up, and still achieve the flavor of most of your favorite fried foods, while using much less oil. I am not doing recipes in this section, but for the sake of clarification will explain these two pan fry photographs.

Thoroughly rinsing then drying chicken pieces (thighs are shown here, but any pieces are okay), hand rubbing olive oil onto the outside surface of each, and then rolling each separate piece in a mixture of flour, salt, and seasoning, is all that is required to prepare them for frying. Picture **B** shows several pieces ready to go into the pan, and picture **C** shows the fried chicken pieces out of the pan and ready to serve. Always let the oil get up to final temperature before carefully placing the chicken pieces in the hot oil. This particular dish was prepared using corn oil, and cooked on medium high setting for approximately 20 minutes, being sure to turn the chicken pieces every 4 or 5 minutes.

A

B

C

Save the earth. It is the only planet with beer, ice cream, and chocolate.

KNUCKLEHEAD NOTES:

Breakfast For a Knucklehead

Bachelor, New Graduate, Beginner, and other Knuckleheads

Breakfast is an unusual heading for a cookbook section, and I realize that. However, since the intent of this cookbook is slightly different than is normal, it seems appropriate to have a section or two that is also different than normal.

Breakfast has to be my favorite meal, and yet I cook it less often than lunch or dinner. A bowl of cereal, a quick cup of coffee, or even a little fast food, snagged on the way to work, is just too convenient in our world of today. However, when you get the time, even if it is just on the weekends, try out some of these simple old-time classics like fried eggs and bacon, or wander into the arena of taste bud enticement with French toast or pancakes. None of these dishes is particularly difficult, and they are guaranteed to start your day off right.

Eggs

Good Morning

Ingredients

Eggs

Vegetable oil

Milk or cream

Salt

1 to 2 eggs are one serving

A Bone from Pennie

The village called and said their idiot is missing, and I think we both know where he is KNUCKLEHEAD.

The scrambled egg recipe is the best way to cook scrambled eggs, and is almost dummy proof. Two main things can go wrong. First, you must make sure the temperature is not above medium; let these eggs cook slowly. Secondly stir frequently. If you do not keep stirring them, the eggs will get brown scorch marks on them, and damage the appearance and taste.

Fried eggs are perhaps the easiest thing to cook for breakfast, and also the most difficult to cook correctly. Be patient, as you will overcook the eggs sometimes, but you will gradually get the hang of it.

Poached eggs are quite easy. Just follow the recipe, and DO NOT forget to add the vinegar to the water.

Always serve eggs immediately after they have cooked. Do not store.

Directions

Use a small storage container, with a very tight sealing lid. Place the container on the work surface, and place 3 to 4 eggs in the container, break the yolks, and salt and season to taste.

Add 1/4 cup of milk or cream. Container should be no more than 1/2 to 2/3 full.

Place the lid on the container, making sure it is secure and tight, and shake vigorously for 15 seconds. Immediately pour the scrambled egg contents into a pan with 1 TBSP of oil, set on **medium** heat. Stir frequently with wooden spoon, to keep brown scorching from occurring, until scrambled eggs are done, as shown in picture **A**. Serve hot.

Picture **B** shows the three most common fried eggs. Sunnyside up is on the far right, over easy is at the bottom left, and over hard is on the top left.

Use a lot of oil, placing about 1/8-inch in the bottom of a flat bottom frying pan. Use a large turner, for flipping the eggs.

Sunnyside up means the egg is not flipped; not even once. Over easy means the egg is flipped one time only. Over hard means there is no soft yolk, and is usually flipped 2 to 3 times. Season all to taste.

Poached eggs are easier to cook than at first it appears, and it is the lowest calorie way of cooking eggs, with no added fat. Using a small sauce pan filled half way with water, bring the water to almost boiling. If the water starts to boil, turn down the heat a small amount. Add 2 TSP of vinegar to the hot water.

Crack an egg into a small measuring cup. Gently pour the egg into the hot water. Use a large slotted spoon to help hold the egg white in close to the yolk. As the egg whites turn to white color, turn off the heat, and cover with lid for 4 minutes. Lift the poached egg out of water with slotted spoon, as shown in picture **C**.

A

B

C

It is imperative in business to know and accept that if there is more than one person in the room, then all is not as it appears.

OMeLet'S

Say Cheese

Ingredients

3 eggs

3 TBSP diced ham

2 TBSP shredded mild cheddar cheese

2 TBSP diced onion

1 TBSP diced sweet red pepper

Seasoning to taste

Serves 2

Note: An omelet pan is shown in pictures. If you do not have one, then use a small sauce pan and flip the circular egg mix into a half circle when the first side is almost done.

A Bone from Pennie

Is there a circus in town? I mean seriously, **KNUCKLeHead**, who dresses you in the morning? Never mind; you will probably get the eggs all over you and have to change clothes anyway.

Undercooking and overcooking are about the only mistakes that can be made with this omelet. Undercooking will leave some raw egg mix on the inside, and is common when you add a lot of extra ingredients and the thickness of the egg mix gets too large. Overcooking is more common, and harder to avoid. I have intentionally shown you picture **C** with one corner of the omelet over cooked and slightly brown, rather than show you a picture perfect omelet. This omelet is still good. If you don't like the look or the taste of a small brown area, simply cut it off and discard. If your guests don't like that, then tell them to go down the road to the nearest diner for breakfast.

Be creative and substitute or use any vegetables, cheeses, or breakfast meats you prefer.

Directions

This particular recipe uses three eggs. You can reduce this to two eggs if you choose.

Accumulate the ingredients shown in picture **A**, prior to beginning the egg mix.

In a small storage container with well sealing lid, crack open and add the eggs. Season to taste, and add 2 TBSP of milk for fluffiness if desired.

Tightly seal the container and shake vigorously for 15 to 20 seconds.

Add all other ingredients, reseal the container, and shake for 5 seconds.

Set the omelet pan on the stove burner, add 1 TBSP of oil, set the temperature to medium, and allow the omelet pan and oil to get up to temperature before proceeding.

Pour the resulting egg, vegetable, and ham mix into one side of the omelet pan, as shown in picture **B**. Allow to cook for about 3 to 4 minutes on one side, or until the first side is firm enough to turn.

Close the omelet pan, by folding the empty side over on top of the side containing the omelet.

Using an oven mitt, hold the two sides together, and quickly invert the pan, causing the omelet mix to now rest in the previously empty side, so that the rest of the omelet can continue cooking.

Cook this side for 3 to 4 minutes, checking periodically for firmness. When the second side has cooked, the omelet is done. Do not try and flip back to the first side for additional cooking, as this will often cause the omelet to burn.

Your completed omelet should appear like the one shown in picture **C**, but with a little luck not contain the small scorched area.

Ⓐ

Ⓑ

Ⓒ

Profanity and loudness usually accompany a weak mind, a weak argument, or both.

Bacon, Ham, Meat

Aces for Atkins

Ingredients

Package of bacon

Large ham slice

Package of sausage

2 to 3 slices of thick sliced bacon, or 3 to 4 slices of thin sliced bacon are one serving.

Allow 1/3 pound of raw ham or sausage as one serving.

A Bone from Pennie

I guess the big question for you KNUCKLEHEAD, is did you escape from the asylum, or are you out on a day pass? I need to know before I trust you cooking bacon in hot grease, which is one of the most dangerous cooking chores we do.

Bacon will fill a pan up when first placed in the skillet, but will shrink significantly as it cooks. This is normal and to be expected.

Ham is baked or cured before being sold, and as such requires very little cooking time. 3 to 4 minutes on each side is satisfactory, unless you want to try and get the edges crispy by cooking a little longer.

Sausage links and sausage patties cook about the same. Raw pork can present some health concerns, so I advise that you go a little well done on sausage, whether links or patties.

Serve all of these while hot, fresh from the skillet.

Directions

There are a huge number of choices when buying bacon. I have a strong preference for *thick sliced*, but just as many people like *thin sliced*. The more white you see in the bacon pieces the more fat in the piece, and the more grease you will have as you cook. Accordingly, the more red or meat that exists in the raw bacon, the less grease, and less shrinkage will occur.

Picture **A** shows bacon frying in a large sauce pan, while the first batch is draining on some paper napkins to the left side of the pan. Notice the draining pieces are substantially smaller than the pieces of bacon frying in the pan.

Picture **B** shows a large piece of bone-in ham that weighs just slightly over 1 pound. This piece of ham can serve 3 or 4 people for breakfast.

I cooked this piece of ham in a sauce pan with ribs on the bottom, as I like the appearance of the dark lines across the ham, for plating appearance. You can just as easily use a flat bottom pan.

Three to four minutes of cooking on each side of the piece of ham, at medium heat, is sufficient to complete this dish and serve the ham.

I have chosen to show you the sausage patties in picture **C**, as they require some preparation (shown in picture), and the links do not.

Place the ground sausage on a cutting board and divide into equal sections of about 1/4 pound each. If desired you may add a small amount of seasoning at this point, but it is not required.

Roll each individual section into a ball, place the ball on the cutting board, and gently press down to form a pancake-like patty about 2 to 3 inches in diameter, and no more than 1/2-inch thick.

Cook each side for 3 to 4 minutes, or until all pink is gone from the center of the patties.

A

B

C

When negotiating, listen more than you speak. You have two ears and only one mouth for a reason.

Breads

Carol's Carb's

Ingredients

1 can of biscuits

*****

1 can of crescent rolls

*****

Sliced bread

Butter

Cinnamon

Sugar

1 piece of any of these is considered one serving.

A Bone from Pennie

Now is as good a time as any, you KNUCKLEHEAD, to remind you that there is a huge difference between golden brown and charcoal black. The main difference being that you can actually eat something that is golden brown.

When you remove either the biscuits or the crescent rolls from the oven, immediately remove the rolls from the tray. The hot tray will actually continue to cook the bottoms of the bread otherwise, and blacken the bottom crust.

Do not grease or spray the cookie trays for either the biscuits or the crescent rolls.

For a little something different, try using white powdered sugar instead of the standard white granular sugar, when making the cinnamon toast. It adds a soft pleasant texture to the piece of toast.

Always serve all three while hot.

Directions

Open the container of biscuits. Depending on what manufacturer you choose, there should be a small tab to pull on the side of the can. Contents are under a small amount of pressure, so expect a small "poof" as you open the can.

Place round sections on a non stick cookie tray. Cook in <u>preheated</u> oven as directed on can. Picture **A** shows 8 biscuits just removed from the oven.

*****

Open the container of crescent rolls. Depending on what manufacturer you choose, there should be a small tab to pull on the side of the can. Contents are under a small amount of pressure, so expect a small "poof" as you open the can.

Crescent dough pieces are triangular in shape. Start from the large end, and roll the dough until you get a layered looking dough roll.

Place rolled sections on a non stick cookie tray, and curve the rolls to form a small crescent. Cook in <u>preheated</u> oven as directed on can. Picture **B** shows 8 crescent rolls just removed from the oven.

*****

I am going to assume you can make toast, so I just wanted to toss in a couple of small twists to add a little extra to your breakfast table.

Put a small amount of butter on your bread before placing the bread slices in the toaster. Keep the butter away from the bottom of the slice, as it will tend to drip down a little as the butter melts.

Picture **C** shows a piece of toast on the left, ready to serve. On the right is a piece of cinnamon toast, made by taking the toast slice out of the toaster, and sprinkling sugar and cinnamon onto the toast.

A

B

C

You cannot be cheated, unless you put yourself in a position to be cheated.

French Toast

Mike's Magic

Ingredients

2 eggs

1/3 cup of milk

1 TBSP cinnamon

2 TBSP of powdered sugar

4 slices of bread

4 TBSP of butter

Serves 4

A Bone from Pennie

My guess, KNUCKLEHEAD, is that your long range plan is to earn big bucks and become wealthy. I think you may do better trying to marry wealthy. That first plan is not looking so good right now.

Once you have placed the dipped bread pieces into the pan, do not try and pour any remaining egg batter onto the top of the cooking French Toast pieces. The batter does not absorb into the saturated bread, and will cook like a scrambled egg.

Do not overcook each side. Notice I use the words golden brown in the recipe text, and do not use the word black. Add some orange zest, any type of fruit jam, or honey as a fun twist.

Variation: Take a grain cereal such as Wheaties or Corn Flakes and crumble them up on a plate. After dipping the bread slices in the egg batter, place them on the cereal flakes to coat and cook same as the original recipe. Very tasty and crunchy.

Directions

Accumulate the ingredients as seen in picture **A**.

Place the eggs, milk, and cinnamon in a container and stir vigorously until well mixed. The cinnamon will tend to clump and stay on the surface, but continue stirring until it is mixed as well as possible.

Pour the liquid into a small square container somewhat similar in size to the size of a slice of bread.

In a large sauce pan place approximately 4 TBSP of butter and melt the butter on medium heat.

When the butter is melted, immediately place one slice of bread into the container with the egg and milk mixture, allowing it to absorb the mixture for about 2 seconds. Flip the slice of bread over for 2 seconds to coat the other side.

Place the slice of battered bread in the pan with the melted butter, and repeat immediately for the other 3 slices, until all 4 slices are in the pan, as shown in picture **B**. Notice the first piece of bread in the top left corner of the pan has more cinnamon on it than the others, which is normal as the first slice of bread absorbs most of the floating cinnamon in the mix. Using the container of ground cinnamon, evenly shake a little cinnamon onto the top surface of the other 3 pieces. Cook on medium.

Cook for 2 minutes, or until bottom surface begins to show light brown patches. Flip each slice, and brown the other side of each piece for about 2 minutes. Repeat for each side once more (brown each side twice for 2 minutes).

Picture **C** shows the final pieces of French Toast, with the surface of each piece a pattern of yellow and golden brown patches, coated with a 1/2 TBSP of powdered sugar on each slice. The top two pieces shown on each plate also have syrup poured on top, which is my favorite way of serving this dish.

A

B

C

Life is tough, but you are tougher. You will find that you can keep going long after you think you can't.

> Sophie's Choice

Pancakes

Ingredients

2 cups of Bisquick mix

1 cup of milk

1 egg

Serves 4

OPTION: I like to add 3 tablespoons of white powdered sugar, and 1 teaspoon of vanilla to the pancake batter, for additional sweetness and flavor.

A Bone from Pennie

Now we know, **Knucklehead**, why in the wild some parents eat their young. Very few things can go wrong with pancakes, but for some reason I'm thinking you may push that envelope.

If your mix is too thick, then add a little bit more milk. Conversely if the mix is too thin, then mix in a little bit more of the dry Bisquick mix.

Make sure you pre-heat the griddle before pouring the pancake mix onto the griddle.

If you are using a non-stick grill, it should not be necessary to use any cooking oil, or PAM; place the mix directly on the hot griddle.

For banana pancakes, mash bananas with a fork, add to the mix, and stir gently. For blueberry, chocolate chip, pecan, etc. you can also add directly to the mix, and *gently* fold the additives into the pancake mix.

Directions

There are numerous recipes for pancakes, that you can make from scratch, but in my opinion using Bisquick mix is the way to go. It is simple, fast, and flavorful.

As you can see from picture **A**, only three ingredients are required to make these pancakes.

Place all ingredients into a large mixing bowl and mix thoroughly. A beater on low speed is best, but if desired use a wisp and stir vigorously. You may end up with a few small lumps when using the wisp, but these will cook out on the griddle.

I suggest you keep the size of your pancakes small, about 4 inches in diameter, as they are much easier to flip. However pancakes are made all the way up to full plate size, 8 to 10 inches being common.

Pre-heat your flat griddle to medium high on stove top.

Ladle the desired quantity of mix onto the hot griddle. Make sure the pancake mix is not too thick, and that the mix flows outward easily to form the desired pancake size. It should not be more than 1/2 inch thick maximum.

Using a flat turner, gently lift up one edge of a pancake after about one minute and check to see if the color is a rich golden brown. Picture **B** shows two pancakes on the right that are ready to be flipped, and on the left are two pancakes that have been flipped one time.

The key to *good* pancakes is to only cook each side one time. Do not keep flipping over and re-cooking each side as this makes the pancakes hard.

Picture **C** shows a serving of one large pancake, buttered, and covered with warm syrup. Pancakes may also be topped with powdered sugar, fresh berries, jams, jellies, etc.

A

B

C

It is a wise man that understands the limits of his knowledge.

19

Waffles

Not Plain Jane

Ingredients

1-3/4 cup of all purpose flour

1-3/4 cup of milk

1 TSP baking soda

1 TSP baking powder

1 TSP sugar

1/8 TSP salt

1/3 cup cooking oil

1/2 TSP vanilla

2 beaten eggs

Makes 4 large waffles

A Bone from Pennie

I have never seen the word "KNUCKLEHEAD" in an obituary, but then you are still kicking, aren't you?

Be sure and let the waffle iron or griddle heat up before placing batter on to cook.

Try using buttermilk instead of plain milk to add a little richness to the mix. You can also substitute soy flour, or unprocessed wheat germ for up to 1/4 cup of each, but make sure the total flour quantity does not go over the 1-3/4 cups specified, or you will end up with a huge dough ball.

You can also substitute melted butter for the oil, to add some richness to the mix.

If you are going to make only one kind of waffle, then add your nuts, blueberries, etc. into the mix before ladling onto the hot grill. If you use blueberries, gently fold the berries into the mix, do not stir, or you will make purple *smurf* waffles, as the blueberries tend to break up easily.

Directions

Crack 2 eggs into a large mixing bowl, and beat.

Add all liquid ingredients and stir well, until mix is uniform throughout.

Add all dry ingredients. Using a beater set on low, mix the ingredients until all lumps are gone and batter has a nice smooth appearance.

The size and type of waffle iron you have, will determine how much batter to place on the griddle. Belgian waffle irons usually require more batter than a standard waffle iron.

Turn on the waffle iron, and wait for the light to come on, indicting the grill is hot and ready for batter to be placed. If you wish to add any extra ingredients such as nuts, bananas, blueberries, etc. make sure you have them prepared and close at hand, as the next step needs to happen quickly.

Ladle approximately one cup of batter onto the preheated grill, and quickly add extra ingredients, and immediately close the lid.

Picture **A** shows one cup of batter on the waffle iron with 1/4 cup of fresh blueberries added on top, and ready to have the lid of the waffle iron closed.

Picture **B** shows a stove top type of griddle iron that makes seven small waffles. You can see that this particular style allows you to make a variety of waffle flavors at one time, such as banana, chopped walnut, half walnut pieces, blueberries, chopped pecans or half pecan pieces.

Waffles are traditionally served with butter and warm syrup. Picture **C** shows my favorite of sprinkled powdered sugar, and warm syrup. Belgian waffles are generally topped with fresh strawberries and whipped cream. You can be bold on this one, and top off your waffles with preferred topping.

A

B

C

Opportunities are seldom lost. Someone will take the ones you let pass you by.

Hash Browns

Hunting Camp

Ingredients

1 large potato

1/2 cup chopped onion

Salt

Pepper

Oil

Serves 2

A Bone from Pennie

Contrary to fraternity lore and myth, KNUCKLEHEAD, onions do not go with everything. However in this case they do complement the dish.

So simple, so easy, so good. There are so many variations of this dish, that I had to choose the one to best help you in the preparation. The potatoes in the pictures are cut about 1/2-inch thick, and that is as thick as you want to cut them, and still be able to get the hash browns cooked all the way through before the potatoes start burning.

Using your grater, you can slice large pieces that are thin, or grate them to the small slivers commonly called shoe string hash browns. Cut the potatoes any way you prefer, just don't go too thick with the pieces.

The onions will usually cook and begin to blacken before the potatoes are done, depending on the thickness of potatoes you prepare. You may want to consider adding the onions later in the cooking process.

Directions

There are very few ingredients in this dish, as shown in picture **A**.

Using a sharp knife, cut the potatoes into pieces of the size you prefer for hash browns. You may use a grater if you like very thin slices, or prefer to grate them into small shoe string pieces. The potatoes may be either skinned or un-skinned, depending on your preference. Finely slice or dice about 1/2 cup of onions.

One large potato will provide enough potato pieces for two servings, but you may wish to cook more servings at one time by simply preparing more potatoes and onions. However do not over load your pan, keeping the layer of vegetables no more than 1-inch thick.

If you have spray vegetable oil, very lightly spray the surface of the cut potatoes and onions before seasoning. This step enables the seasoning to stick to the vegetable pieces more readily. Salt and pepper may be added to the vegetable pieces before placing in the pan, as shown in picture **B**, which I recommend if you are using the vegetable spray, or you may season the pieces in the pan as you begin cooking.

Add 2 TBSP of vegetable oil to a large sauce pan, and set the heat to medium. Add the potatoes and onions that you have already prepared, and leave uncovered. Drizzle one TBSP of vegetable oil over the top of the vegetables. You will need to use a flat turner to *flip* the pieces over, every 2 or 3 minutes, as they cook. Stirring with a spoon, will not as effectively brown each side of the pieces.

Depending on the thickness of the potato pieces you have prepared, it will take 15 to 20 minutes to prepare this dish. Be sure to continually flip and turn the pieces as they brown, and do not over cook. Hash browns should be a rich golden brown, with dark brown edges, as shown in picture **C**, and should be soft on the inside, and not firm or raw.

Wisdom is not just speaking and sharing your thoughts, but often knowing when to keep your mouth shut.

KNUCKLEHEAD NOTES:

Salads For a Knucklehead

Bachelor, New Graduate, Beginner, and other Knuckleheads

*Almost everyone loves a good salad; **good** being the operative word here. I know you can handle the everyday tossed salad, so I have endeavored to put some salad recipes in this section, that you may not have seen, or are perhaps a little more uncommon in cookbooks.*

First, it is imperative that you have fresh, crisp lettuce and fresh, juicy fruits and vegetables. If you don't have those, then your final dish will not be the success you had hoped for. Secondly, take the time to add a little art and craftsmanship into the appearance of your salad dishes. Appearance makes a huge difference in how people perceive the dish and, oddly enough, how they perceive it to taste as well. Make these dishes appealing, you **Knucklehead**; *it doesn't take any more effort to do it right than to just throw it together.*

Broccoli Salad

Palmetto's Finest

Ingredients

1 pound bacon (thick slices)

3 heads (bunches) of broccoli

6 boiled eggs

3/4 cup mild cheddar cheese

1 cup Miracle Whip dressing

1/4 cup red wine vinegar

1/2 cup sugar

1/4 cup diced red onions

1 TSP salt

1 TSP ground pepper

Serves 8

A Bone from Pennie

If cooking was a battle of wits, you KNUCKLEHEAD, you would probably have to surrender to one of these broccoli florets or a large zucchini. I know there is intelligent life here on earth, which just makes me think that you may be a visitor.

Slice away, and discard, all but about 1 inch of the stalk on the broccoli. When preparing the broccoli cut the florets into about 3 pieces each.

Do not burn the bacon, but try to get it as crisp as possible to facilitate crumbling it onto the salad.

Slice the eggs one time with the egg slicer and then place them in the salad. As you stir the mixture of ingredients, the eggs will crumble to bite size pieces.

The heads of broccoli differ in size from different stores and different times of the season. You need approximately 2 pounds of broccoli.

Directions

Fry one pound of bacon and place to the side. Once cool, crumble it into small pieces.

Prepare the broccoli bunches by slicing them into bite size pieces. As you cut up the broccoli, individual broccoli florets will come apart that are about the size of half a ping pong ball. These should be cut into halves or thirds, to give you an idea of size. Reference the chopped pieces shown in picture **A**.

Peel the six boiled eggs, and discard the shells. Place them on an egg slicer one time only, and place to the side.

Dice a red onion to obtain 1/4 cup diced onion.

Using a 2 cup measuring container, pour in the vinegar, sugar, salt, pepper, and Miracle Whip dressing. Stir well. You may wish to pour the ingredients into a lidded container and shake vigorously to mix. There will be small lumps of Miracle Whip on the surface, and that is okay.

You should now have all the ingredients accumulated, as shown in picture **B**.

Place all of the non-liquid ingredients (broccoli pieces, crumbled bacon, sliced eggs, onions, and cheese) into a large salad bowl, reference picture **C**, cover with sealable lid or saran wrap, and refrigerate until ready to serve.

Place the container of salad dressing in the refrigerator to chill as well.

When ready to serve, remove the lid to the salad bowl, and pour the entire container of dressing onto the prepared salad. Gently and slowly fold the salad mix with the dressing to avoid breaking up the ingredients more than necessary.

Serve as salad or as side dish to entrée.

A

B

C

Keep your words soft and tender, as you may have to eat them later on.

Tomato Capri

> Lee's Mad Mix

Ingredients

1 cup small cherry tomatoes

1/4 cup olive oil

1/4 cup Tantillo Balsamic Bliss glaze

1/2 cup shredded mozzarella cheese.

1 TSP salt

Serves 2

A Bone from Pennie

I finally figured out what you remind me of KNUCKLEHEAD; a door stop that eats, and thinks cooking is unpleasant. Cooking is not unpleasant. A two finger prostate exam is unpleasant. Cooking and preparing food is fun, so loosen up there pork chop.

If you do not have the specific Tantillo Balsamic Bliss glaze that I have listed in the recipe, then you may substitute a basic balsamic vinegar.

Pour the balsamic glaze onto the cheese before adding the olive oil, to prevent the olive oil from coating the cheese, and restricting the penetration of the balsamic flavoring.

You can use any type of olive oil, but cold pressed virgin olive oil is the best. A light olive oil works, but is somewhat overwhelmed with the balsamic vinegar, and is unable to add much to the flavor. However the olive oils with additives, such as basil, are excellent on this dish.

Directions

Accumulate the four base ingredients for this simple salad as shown in picture **A**.

Slice the tomatoes into halves, or bite size pieces depending on the type of tomatoes you purchased. Picture **B** shows one cup of cherry tomatoes split in half.

Place the tomatoes on a flat bottom salad bowl or small plate and evenly distribute around the plate.

Add salt, but not very much as the glaze has some salt in its ingredients.

Sprinkle the shredded mozzarella cheese over the tomatoes and in between so as to somewhat cover the entire plate.

Drizzle the Tantillo Balsamic Bliss onto the tomatoes and shredded cheese.

Drizzle the olive oil onto the mix, making sure to get some on each piece of tomato.

The salad is complete. I suggest you serve immediately, but you can refrigerate it for a short time, but the cheese has a tendency to become dry.

The completed salad is shown on the left side of picture **C**.

Since this recipe was so simple and short, I also prepared the same dish, using slices of large tomatoes, and small mozzarella balls called *pearls*. The dish is traditionally served as tomato slices with sliced fresh mozzarella on top. Although I have never seen it served with the shredded mozzarella in this recipe, I find the shredded cheese is far better than the slices or pearls of mozzarella, in that the shredded mozzarella cheese absorbs and holds the Balsamic Bliss.

A

B

C

The difficult choice is usually the right choice. Be strong and do the right thing.

Orange Tart Salad

Botzum's Best

Ingredients

1/2 cup sliced almonds

3 TBSP white sugar

*****

1 TSP both salt and pepper

1/2 cup olive oil

2 TBSP finely chopped fresh parsley

4 TBSP sugar

4 TBSP vinegar

1 TBSP Tabasco sauce

*****

4 servings of lettuce (any type)

1 cup finely chopped celery

1/2 cup finely chopped green shallots

14 oz. can chilled mandarin oranges

Serves 4

A Bone from Pennie

Well, well, well, KNUCKLeHead. Aren't you just cuter than a duck wearing a hat. You should instead wear a *Do-Not-Disturb sign* around your neck as you are obviously quite disturbed enough, to be trying to prepare a salad this classy.

You must continually stir the almond and sugar mixture. Sugar burns easily and quickly, and will ruin the preparation if over heated.

Make sure you drain the mandarin oranges, and use only the segments, and not the juice.

The quantities on the dressing are not overly critical. If you like a little extra zip then add some extra Tabasco sauce. If you don't like the acidic flavor of the vinegar or the oiliness of the olive oil, then slightly reduce those quantities.

All of the ingredients, except for the almonds, should be chilled before serving.

Directions

In a small sauce pan over medium heat, add almonds and sugar, and cook slowly with *continuous* stirring, until the almonds are browned and sugar coated.

Picture **A** shows the raw almond slivers on the left, and the sugar coated cooked almonds on the right. No need to overcook. Once the almonds have turned a darker brown, and most of the sugar has adhered, they are done.

*****

Prepare all the ingredients for the dressing, place in a storage container with good sealing lid, and shake vigorously. Chill in refrigerator for one hour, or overnight if possible.

Dressing is shown in picture **B** in a small serving bowl, for presentation purposes only. The ingredients in the dressing do not mix together well, and will separate when left standing. When you remove the dressing from the refrigerator, there will be three distinct layers of ingredients. Shake the container well, and pour dressing out immediately onto the salads.

*****

Prepare all of the salad ingredients, and place lettuce, celery, and onions in a large mixing bowl. Gently toss to evenly mix components.

Remove salad mixture to four serving bowls.

Top each with mandarin orange slices.

Top each with sugar coated roasted almonds.

Shake up dressing mixture and pour immediately onto the salads.

Picture **C** shows one serving in a small serving bowl.

A

B

C

Great love and great achievement, usually involve great risk.

Egg Salad

For Pickle Slicers

Ingredients

4 hard boiled eggs

2 TBSP sweet pickle relish

2 small sweet peppers

1/3 cup Miracle Whip

Pinch of salt

1 TSP paprika

1 1/2 TBSP plain yellow mustard

Lettuce

Sandwich bread

Serves 3

A Bone from Pennie

My wish for you KNUCKLEHEAD, is that we were in Oz, and the wizard had two brains to give out instead of one. Maybe then you would get smart enough to start paying attention.

I try to use two different colored peppers, an orange and a red one is shown in the pictures, so as to add some color to the salad. Any type of pepper is fine including the more common large sweet green peppers, from which the appropriate and proportional amount of pepper can be cut and added, in lieu of the small peppers shown.

Refrigerate and store the balance of the green peppers for future use in other recipes. Peppers kept in a sealed storage container can be kept for at least a week or so, and not thrown away or wasted.

Other mustards can be substituted, but dramatically change the taste and character of this traditional egg salad dish.

Directions

This is a very simple recipe requiring very few ingredients, as shown in picture **A**.

Peel the boiled eggs, then using an egg slicer, double slice the eggs and place in a medium sized mixing bowl or storage bowl container.

Slice the peppers into small pieces or small slivers, and add to the bowl.

Thinly slice the shallots and add to the bowl.

Lightly salt the surface of the ingredients.

Add both the sweet relish, mustard, and Miracle Whip dressing to the ingredients in the bowl.

Picture **B** shows the sample recipe with all of the ingredients in the bowl.

Gently fold, do not stir, the ingredients together, trying not to break up the egg pieces any more than necessary, until you have a uniform mix of all ingredients.

Picture **C** depicts two different ways to serve the dish. On the left is the egg salad served on a bed of lettuce as a salad course. On the right demonstrates the egg salad used to make an egg salad sandwich.

Egg salad can safely be refrigerated in a sealed container, and stored for 2 or 3 days.

Arguing with a woman is like wrestling with a pig in the mud. You both get dirty, and after a while you find out the pig actually enjoys it.

27

Tuna Salad

Shannon's Shot

Ingredients

3 boiled eggs

1 12oz. Can Albacore tuna

1 cup Miracle Whip dressing

1/2 cup sweet relish

1/8 teaspoon of salt

Serves approx. 6

Note: I highly recommend that you only buy and use <u>albacore</u> tuna. Some of the cheaper tuna meats can just smell awful, and can ruin this dish even if properly prepared.

A Bone from Pennie

Pay attention here KNUCKLEHEAD, cause if you don't, this conglomeration is going to smell and taste like cat spit and sulphur, with just a hint of wet dog blended in.

I like to use a storage bowl, in lieu of mixing bowl, so that I can immediately seal with a lid and store in the refrigerator until ready to serve.

Do not stir the ingredients, as this will break up the tuna into small flaky pieces, and detract from the texture of the dish. Gently fold.

You may want to use a salt shaker to spread the little bit of salt required, so as to avoid getting concentrated areas of salt that does not distribute well with the folding.

Bib lettuce is recommended with either the sandwich serving or the salad serving.

Eggs shown in picture **A** are double sliced on egg slicer.

Directions

In a medium sized mixing bowl or storage bowl, place the drained tuna, Miracle Whip, and relish. Lightly distribute salt over the mixture. Use an egg slicer, or simply mash with a fork, to slice the boiled eggs and place them in the bowl as well. Using a large spoon or spatula gently fold the ingredients (do not stir vigorously) until all ingredients are mixed into one evenly distributed mix. Serve on bread as sandwich, or serve on bed of lettuce as a salad.

Variations:

This particular recipe makes a relatively sweet sandwich spread. Dill pickle relish may be equally substituted for the sweet relish, and likewise mayonnaise may be equally substituted for the Miracle Whip. Either of these changes, or both in conjunction with each other, will remove some of the sweetness.

If you wish to kick it up a notch, you may add a dash of cayenne pepper or ground peppercorns.

Tuna sandwiches are often served with a leaf of lettuce, and or sliced tomatoes. Tomatoes are also commonly used to garnish a scoop of tuna salad when it is served as a salad, usually on a bed of lettuce.

All of these variations are cooks preference.

A

B

C

Whether you think you can or can't; You are correct.

Mandarin Orange

Author's Favorite

Ingredients

2 servings of loose leaf lettuce

1 can of mandarin oranges (drained)

1/3 cup chopped English walnuts

1 jar of Brianna's poppy seed dressing

2 fresh scallions

Serves 2

A Bone from Pennie

Frankly **KNUCKeHead**, I think your mother should have smothered you in the crib, as she just hasn't left me much to work with here.

You can use whole walnuts if you choose, or crumble them to get larger pieces than the chopped.

I find that the Brianna's poppy seed dressing is the absolute best for this dish, but any sweet poppy seed type dressing is fine.

Any type of lettuce can be substituted as well. I have used *spring mix* that can be purchased in bags at the grocery store, which lets me use some of the color available in that mix for plating appearance.

Cut the scallions very thin and distribute evenly on the salad.

A large can of mandarin oranges will allow you to make four servings at once, keeping all the rest of the ingredients doubled in proportion.

Directions

Accumulate all of your ingredients as shown in picture **A**.

Place the loose leaf lettuce in the salad bowls in which the dish will be served. If you choose to use a lettuce with some color in it, try to arrange the pieces of lettuce to make the salad look more appealing.

Add the chopped nuts to the center of the arranged lettuce without disturbing the arrangement.

Sprinkle the scallions around the top surface of the lettuce mix.

In picture **B** I have tried to add a little artistic flair to the dish by placing the mandarin oranges in four distinct piles along the outside of the bowl. If you prefer you may evenly distribute the mandarin oranges around the top surface of the salad, or better yet come up with your own artistic arrangement of the lettuce and oranges. The arrangement is for plating appearance only, as it all tastes the same, but a pretty dish is so much nicer to serve than one randomly thrown together.

Cover the dish with saran wrap until ready to serve, and chill in the refrigerator for up to two hours.

When ready to serve, remove the salad dishes from the refrigerator, uncover, and drizzle the salad dressing around the top of the salad. Do not mix and stir. The salad is now ready to serve, and should appear something like the two salads shown in picture **C**.

This particular salad is so sweet and refreshing, it is best served as a separate course in advance of the main meal, rather than as a side salad in conjunction with the main course.

A

B

C

You have a conscience, and should you forget that, it will remind you again and again.

Five Cup Salad

Jewell's Gem

Ingredients

1 cup coconut

1 cup sour cream

1 cup crushed pineapple (drained)

1 cup mandarin orange slices (drained)

1 cup miniature marshmallows

Maraschino cherries (optional)

Serves 6 to 8

A Bone from Pennie

This dish is so simple it is nearly impossible to not mix correctly. So simple even a KNUCKLEHEAD can do it.

The most common mistake made in the preparation of this dish, is not draining the mandarin oranges and the crushed pineapple. That excess juice makes the salad too runny.

Remember that one cup is equal to 8 ounces. The sour cream, mandarin oranges, and pineapple pieces for instance can usually be purchased in containers of that size which keeps you from having to measure. Just dump the contents of an 8 ounce container directly into the mixing bowl.

Quantities are not overly crucial in this salad. For instance, I like mandarin oranges so I increased the mandarin orange content up to 12 ounces. The same is true for the other components as well.

This dish is absolutely wonderful.

Directions

Procure 1 cup each of the five main ingredients, as shown in picture **A**.

I suggest you use a storage bowl to mix in. However if you plan on setting the salad dish on the table then use an attractive serving bowl.

Place all 5 ingredients one cup at a time into the bowl. Using a wooden spoon or soft spatula, fold the ingredients together, being careful not to break up the mandarin oranges. This mixing should take about 2 to 3 minutes

When complete with mixing, the dish is ready to serve or to refrigerate for serving later. You will have 5 cups of salad, as shown in picture **B**, which can serve six to eight people easily.

This dish can be served as a salad on separate plate from the entrée, or as a side dish to the entrée. It is sweet enough to also serve as a dessert if you so choose.

If you elect to serve the dish as a separate salad, as I have done in picture **C**, then you may wish to garnish the dish after plating. Place 3 or 4 maraschino cherries on top of the salad, and then spread about a tablespoon of loose coconut over the top. This will add some color and some texture, and make a much more appealing dish to view.

As an option, you may take the maraschino cherries, cut them in half, and blend them into the salad as well. About one half cup of cherries is plenty.

A

B

C

Every man is your teacher, in that you may learn from him. Every man.

Kraut Salad

Berger's Blast

Ingredients

1- 32 oz. jar of sauerkraut

1/2 cup- diced celery

1/2 cup- diced onion

1/2 cup- diced peppers

1 cup- sugar

1/3 cup- vinegar

Serves 8

A Bone from Pennie

Yes this recipe is *simple* KNUCKLEHEAD, but frankly so are you. It can be screwed up and I hope to keep you from doing that. Now pay attention.

This dish is excellent to serve with spicy or hot fried foods. It cuts the grease and allows your mouth to recover and better taste each following bite. It also neutralizes spicy flavors such as onions and peppers to enhance the flavor.

You can use any onions and peppers, but try to use some that have a deep color to them, as they make the salad so much more appealing to the eye.

Constantly stir the sugar and vinegar mix, and do not let it scorch or burn. Remember that sugar wants to caramelize and has a tendency to burn easily, which will make you lose your temper, and possibly a pot as well.

This salad dish is a surprise; it does not taste like sauerkraut, and is very sweet and tangy.

Directions

Make sure you have all the ingredients shown in picture **A**.

Chop 1/2 cup red onion

Chop 1/2 cup celery

Chop 1/2 cup red, orange, or green sweet peppers.

Place a colander in the sink, and pour all of the sauerkraut into the colander. Run cold water over the kraut to thoroughly rinse all the juice off the kraut.

In a large sealable container/mixing bowl, place the kraut, peppers, onions, and celery, and mix well. Temporarily set the salad aside.

Using a small sauce pan, with a temperature setting of medium, add the sugar and vinegar only to the pan, and continually stir for about 4 to 5 minutes. The liquid should come to a slow boil, and become somewhat clear.

Pour the vinegar and sugar mix over the contents in the bowl and mix thoroughly. Cover the bowl with sealable lid similar to picture **B**, and set in the refrigerator to chill overnight.

Serve as salad in dish, or as a side dish on the plate with entrée. Picture **C** shows a portion of the final salad in a small salad bowl, ready to serve.

A

B

C

When you need a helping hand, look first at the end of your own arm.

KNUCKLEHEAD NOTES:

Entrée's For a Knucklehead

Bachelor, New Graduate, Beginner, and other Knuckleheads

    This section is the reason I gained 25 pounds while preparing this book. Entrées are my favorite type of dish to cook, and I have included my favorite recipes that I have accumulated over the years. Don't miss my barbecued ribs recipe.

    There are several **DO'S** and **DON'T'S** to learn. **DO** read and carefully follow the directions. **DO** buy high-quality meats and produce. **DO** be careful around hot grease and hot stove-tops and ovens. **DON'T** be afraid to try any of these dishes; if I can do them successfully, so can you. **DON'T** guess at measurements and amounts. **DON'T** forget to think and apply logic as you go through the recipes. And above all else, **DON'T** forget to kiss the one you love.

Spaghetti

Springfield Spice

Ingredients

1 pound ground beef

1 pound ground Italian sausage

1/2 cup diced onion

1/4 cup minced garlic

26 oz. jar of pasta sauce

1/2 TSP garlic salt

1/4 TSP ground pepper

1/2 TSP all purpose seasoning

1 TBSP brown sugar

Note: About 2 to 3 ounces of pasta is considered one serving.

Dish serves 6 easily.

A Bone from Pennie

I have heard it said, KNUCKLEHEAD, that it is better to be silent and be thought a fool, than to speak and remove all doubt. You, however, may speak, as we have no doubt.

When you add the beef and sausage to the pan, it will be in large chunks. Use a wooden spoon to break it up into smaller pieces while you are browning and stirring the meats.

If the ground meat and sausage are lean then there will be very little residual oil in the browned meat. If, however, you use meats with more fat, then a lot of oil will develop and you may wish to drain that oil off and discard, before pouring in the sauce.

Most types of sausage have seasoning in them, and so be careful of over doing it when you add your seasoning after browning.

You may add some tomato sauce if you like a little more acidic flavor, or eliminate the brown sugar for same.

Directions

Accumulate all of the ingredients before getting started (picture **A**). Place the ground beef and sausage in large sauce pan and brown on medium heat. Do not over brown the meat at this stage, as it will continue to cook later when the sauce is added. Sausage often has an orange appearance, and the ground beef more of a reddish tone, as shown in picture **B**. Add the garlic and onions at about the halfway point of browning. The later you add them the firmer they will be in the final dish.

Browning is complete once all of the orange and red color of the meats has become a light brown. Do not allow the meat to get dark brown edges or it will become tough and develop an undesirable texture. After browning leave the meat on the burner and add the jar of pasta sauce. Immediately go to the sink and fill the jar up with water, about half way, apply the jar lid back on the jar and shake a few times to dissolve the balance of the sauce in the jar into the water mixture, and then pour the water into the meat and sauce in the sauce pan.

Allow the mixture to come back to a low boil and remain boiling for about 5 minutes in the uncovered sauce pan. Turn back the heat to a low or simmer setting so that just a few small bubbles are coming up to the surface of the sauce, and then cover with tight fitting lid and cook for 20 to 30 minutes.

While the sauce is simmering, prepare the pasta you wish to use for the dish, according to the directions I have given you on page 10 of this book. Pour the cooked pasta into a colander set in the sink and gently rinse with warm water.

Place a serving of pasta on a serving plate, and carefully ladle the sauce into the center of the pasta, as shown in picture **C**, and serve while hot.

Both the sauce and the pasta can be stored in a sealed container in the refrigerator for 3 or 4 days.

A

B

C

If stupidity got you in the mess, then try thinking your way out.

Chili Con Fuego

Emily's Excellence

Ingredients

1 Package Chili mix

2 pounds lean ground meat

1 can (14-16 ounce) diced tomatoes

1 can (14-16 ounce) tomato sauce

1 can (14-16 ounce) chili beans

1/2 onion diced

1/4 cup diced peppers (any kind)

3 TBSP minced garlic

Serves 6 to 8

A Bone from Pennie

I have seen rats scurrying out of a burning meth lab that looked more organized than you do KNUCKLeHead. Settle down and follow the recipe.

Do not brown the meat on high as it will make the meat hard and chewy.

You may substitute real slices of fresh garlic in place of the minced garlic, if desired. If you use large pieces of garlic, then add them in the pan at the same time you start browning the meat, rather than at the half way point.

For a slightly different taste, use one pound lean ground meat and one pound ground sausage. This adds a little zip to the chili. Try not to cook the chili for more than 30 minutes as it tends to toughen up the ground meat.

Add a teaspoon of red chili powder, or a few drops of Tabasco sauce, just before you cover it to cook for 30 minutes.

Directions

Make sure you have all the ingredients available as shown in picture **A**.

In a large sauce pan add 2 to 3 TBSP of oil, and place the meat in the pan to begin browning on medium heat, as shown in picture **B**. Browning should take about 8 to 10 minutes at this setting.

About half way thru the browning, add the onions, peppers, and garlic, and stir in well. The onion pieces should remain somewhat firm.

Open the pack of seasoning and spread evenly across the surface of the browned meat. Allow to set on the surface of the meat a minute or so before stirring in to the ingredients.

Open all three cans (chili beans, diced tomatoes, and tomato sauce) and pour into the pan on top of the meat. Stir in slowly so as not to break up the beans. Fill the empty can of tomato sauce with water, swirling the water around as you fill the can to get all the paste out, and add this to the mix.

Allow the mix to come back to a slow boil, still on the medium heat, and cook for 5 minutes

Turn the heat down to low, cover the pan with a tight fitting lid, and cook for 30 minutes. The dish is now complete and ready to serve, and should appear similar to the completed chili dish shown in picture **C**.

Use a ladle to remove the chili and place in bowls. Serve while hot.

Mild cheddar cheese sprinkled on top as a garnish, or some thin slivers of fresh onions and peppers added on top for plating appearance, are both excellent garnishes for this dish. Thin slices of jalapeno peppers are also a good garnish.

Serve hot in small bowls, with saltine crackers.

Always have a Plan B. Be willing to live with the Plan B results if you have to, or get an entirely new game plan altogether.

Pot Roast

Hartville Style

Ingredients

1 pot roast 2 to 3 pounds

3 to 4 small red potatoes

1 cup raw carrots

Paprika

Parsley flakes

Seasoning

Serves 4 to 6

A Bone from Pennie

Just about now you are thinking about ordering a pizza or Chinese take-out, you KNUCKLEHEAD. Stop being pessimistic; that has never helped anyone produce a successful result in any endeavor.

The key to this entire simple recipe is selecting a good cut of meat. A seven bone pot roast is shown here, and any cut of meat that includes the words *pot roast* should be fine.

Slice or cut the potatoes to a size of about 3 or 4 bites, keeping them at least 1/2-inch thick.

The aluminum foil shown in the red Dutch oven cooking pot is simply for clean up purposes. It is not required, but it does make clean up a lot faster and simpler.

If you have olive oil spray, it is perfect for use on the vegetables, to hold the parsley and paprika onto the separate pieces.

Directions

Picture **A** shows the various ingredients necessary to cook this dish.

Pre-heat oven to 550 degrees (Broil setting), while you are preparing the recipe.

Trim the pot roast if necessary, so that it fits into the bottom of the Dutch oven pot, with room on the sides of the meat for the vegetables later.

Coat one side of the pot roast with olive oil, and season liberally with garlic salt, all purpose seasoning, and ground black pepper, rubbing and pressing the seasoning into the meat.

Place the pot roast into the pot, seasoned side down, and repeat the olive oil and seasoning process on the top side, while in the pot.

Cut the potatoes and carrots on a cutting board and lightly coat with olive oil. Sprinkle both with parsley flakes seasoning, and paprika. Place the potato and carrot pieces individually (one at a time) into the pot alongside the pot roast, as shown in picture **B**, trying to get all of them in the pot and alongside the roast.

Securely cover the pot with the lid, and place in the pre-heated oven at 550 degrees for 30 minutes, being sure to set the timer.

When the timer sounds, turn the oven OFF. Do not open the oven to look at the dish, but set the timer again for 45 minutes, allowing the dish to continue to cook in the now declining temperature in the oven.

When the timer sounds the second time the pot roast is ready to serve. Remove the pot and set on stove top or pot holder, and serve within 15 minutes. Picture **C** shows the completed dish on a serving plate.

A

B

C

Have courage. Never let the fear of failure keep you from succeeding.

BBQ Baby Back Ribs

For Daniel

Ingredients

1 rack baby-back ribs (3 pounds+)

1 bottle of BBQ spice rub

1 bottle BBQ sauce

Olive oil

Serves 2 to 4

A Bone from Pennie

I'm going to warn you right now KNUCKLEHEAD, don't eat these ribs in the dark. They are so good, that if you start dripping sauce down your hands, I think you may chew your arms off right up to your elbows.

The good news about this recipe is that you can use any quantity of meat you choose to purchase. The recipe remains the same for any quantity, and it involves only 4 ingredients.

Once again I show the baking dish lined with aluminum foil, but this is done only for clean up purposes and is not a requirement to cook this recipe.

Broiling happens very quick. Use the oven light to illuminate the ribs in the last step when they are broiling uncovered, so that you can be sure they do not burn. The proximity to the actual heating coil in the top of the oven can easily change the broiling time by 1 or 2 minutes.

Directions

Pre-heat the oven to 550 degrees (Broil).

Unwrap the baby-back ribs from store packaging, and rinse in cold water. Dab dry with towel or paper towel.

Lightly coat all surfaces of the ribs with olive oil. If preferred you may use an olive oil spray, rather than handling the meat.

After applying the oil, sprinkle the meat side (one side of ribs is bone, and the other side is meat) with a dry spice rub, and then using your fingers, massage the spice rub into the meaty surface of the ribs. Picture **A** shows a small section of ribs, properly prepared and placed in a baking container that is oven safe. I have used The Salt Lick dry spice rub and BBQ sauce (my absolute favorites) in this recipe, as seen in the pictures, but your favorite brand or substitution is fine.

Place the seasoned meat in an oven safe pan or baking dish, and tightly seal with either a lid or aluminum foil. I usually use aluminum foil.

Place the dish in the pre-heated oven and set the timer for 50 minutes.

When the timer sounds, turn the oven OFF. Do not open the oven door to check on the meat, but rather set the timer for an additional 50 minutes, allowing the ribs to continue to cook in decelerating temperature.

When timer sounds, remove the dish to the stove top, and immediately re-set the oven for 550 degrees (Broil).

While waiting for the oven to come back up to temperature, allow the ribs to cool for a few minutes, then baste the top surface only, very lightly, with BBQ sauce, using a basting brush shown in picture **B**.

Place the ribs back in the oven on the top shelf, <u>uncovered,</u> and broil the ribs for 6 minutes, or until top surface is rich golden brown. Do not burn.

Remove dish from oven, and allow to cool for 4 or 5 minutes, then coat the top surface liberally with the BBQ sauce you have chosen, and serve. Picture **C** shows the broiled section of ribs on the right after broiling, and the sauce covered ribs on the left.

A

B

C

Memorize these words to heart; "Thank you" and "I'm sorry". Use them often.

37

BBQ Cola Ribs

> Runner-up Ribs

Ingredients

1 rack of ribs (any kind)

2 liters of coca-cola

BBQ sauce.

Serves 2 to 4

A Bone from Pennie

Personally KNUCKLEHEAD, I find your interest in my cookbook, inspiring if not flattering. However, professionally I find it a little disturbing and scary.

The limited ingredients, make this an easy recipe to prepare, but it is a little time consuming with the cooling time, so be sure and leave yourself enough time to properly prepare this meal.

You will note that the recipe has not used any spices or seasoning, relying only on the flavors absorbed in the meat from the coca-cola. This is a very mild and pleasing recipe without any additional seasoning. If you desire a spicier rib flavor, then apply your seasoning after the boiling process, and before chilling the ribs.

The color and appearance of the boiling ribs is rather odd and different. Do not be alarmed, as this is simply to be expected and quite normal.

Directions

Unwrap the ribs from store packaging, and rinse in cold water. Dab dry with towel or paper towel.

Cut the ribs into either one rib or two rib pieces, using a sharp knife and cutting board.

On the stove top, place a large stock pot that can hold at least 1 gallon of liquid or more, and pour in the coca-cola. Set the heat at medium, after the coca-cola is in the pot.

While the liquid is beginning to heat, add all the ribs to the coca-cola liquid. At this point you should not have the liquid within 3 or 4 inches of the top, because as the liquid begins to boil, a foam will form that will bubble over the edges, if room is not available at the top of the pot.

Bring the liquid to a rolling boil, reference picture **A**, and hold for 15 minutes.

Turn the heat down to obtain a slow bubbling boil, cover with a lid, and boil slowly for an additional 75 minutes.

Remove the pot from the stove top, using oven mitts or pot holders, and pour the entire contents into a colander in the sink, allowing the liquid to be totally discarded.

Ribs should be orange/brown in color, as shown in picture **B**, and be well cooked throughout.

Place the ribs in a sealed container, and preferably chill overnight in the refrigerator. If unable to chill overnight then try and put them in the refrigerator for at least 1 to 2 hours.

About 30 minutes before you are ready to serve the ribs, remove them from the refrigerator, and place them in a large sauce pan, on medium high heat, and using 2 TBSP of olive oil in the pan, sear and brown the ribs to crisp the outer surface of the ribs on all sides.

Remove the ribs with tongs, and place on serving plate and coat liberally with barbecue sauce of your choice.

Picture **C** shows the seared ribs on the right, and the picture on the left shows the ribs after coating with the BBQ sauce, and ready to serve.

A

B

C

If you find yourself in a hole, the first thing to do is to stop digging.

Steak in a Pan

Thanks Van

Ingredients

2 rib eye steaks

Seasoning

Butter

Olive oil

Serves 2

A Bone from Pennie

I hope to bump into you someday Knucklehead; assuming you are in front of a wood chipper.

First and foremost to cooking good steaks, is to buy high quality good cuts of meat. I use rib eyes for almost all of my meat entrée's, as a personal choice, but porterhouse, and T-bone cuts are perfect for this type of pan frying as well.

Watch for specials and sales at your grocer, and you can purchase high quality cuts for about the same price as cheaper cuts on a regular day at the store.

If you really want to clog those arteries, add some additional butter to the pan when cooking the second side of each steak, making sure to get it under the steaks, and not just to the sides of the steak.

Warning: You will never want to cook steaks outside on the grill again, after using this recipe.

Directions

The two steaks shown in picture **A** are boneless rib eyes that are 12 ounces each and just less than one inch thick.

To prepare the steaks, lightly coat both sides with olive oil. Sprinkle the seasoning onto the steaks, and gently massage the seasoning into the steak with your fingers. Flip the steaks over and repeat for the second side as well.

When you are finished, you should have two steaks similar in appearance to the two seasoned steaks in picture **B**.

The pan I use for steaks, has ribs on the bottom, as I like the appearance of the dark lines across the steak, which makes it look like the steaks have been grilled. A flat bottomed large sauce pan is fine for this recipe, and will in fact give a full even *crust* on the steak, which you do not get with the ribs on the pan.

Place the pan on the stove top, set the heat to medium, and place a half stick of butter in the pan to melt. Do not over heat or scorch the butter, just get it melted.

Just as the butter completes melting, place the steaks in the pan and turn the heat up to medium high. You will only cook each side **one time**, so sneak a peek at the bottom of one of the steaks after 2 or 3 minutes to see if it is close to the level of cooking (rare, medium, well-done, etc.) that you desire. When you are satisfied with the steaks' appearance, flip the steaks over and repeat for the other sides.

The two steaks shown in picture **C** were cooked for 4 minutes on each side, on medium high heat, and were *medium*. The steaks shown in this picture are complete and ready to be served, straight out of the pan to the serving plate.

Forget revenge and hatred. It is the venom that kills, not the bite.

Beef Tips

A la Noodles

Ingredients

1.5 pounds rib eye steak cut in pieces

1/2 cup olive oil

2 TBSP brown sugar

2 TBSP all purpose seasoning

1 TBSP minced garlic

1/2 TBSP garlic salt

1 TBSP Dijon mustard

*****

2 TBSP Worcestershire sauce

1 cup fresh mushrooms

3 TBSP butter

1 bottle regular beer (not light)

4 servings of noodles

Serves 4

A Bone from Pennie

This dish is prepared by many chef's. However to call you a chef, KNUCKLE-HEAD, just somehow seems wrong. It reminds me of a dog I once had that had one ear, one gonad, three legs, and was blind in one eye. His name was Lucky.

For a thicker gravy, add a tablespoon of corn starch when you add the mushrooms.

Use a pan that allows all of the meat pieces to sit on the bottom, and not stack up on top of each other. This helps keep the meat moist while it is braising.

The brown sugar in the spice and oil mix will cause the beef tips to brown quickly and tend to get a little black sometimes, depending on the length of time you keep them on the heat.

Do not overcook this dish, as that will cause the meat to become tough.

Any high quality beef, preferably with heavy marbling, can be used.

Directions

Make sure you have all the ingredients as listed, and also shown in picture **A**, before starting.

Use a storage container with a good sealable lid that can hold about 1-1/2 to 2 times the volume of meat. Place the first six ingredients in the container in any order, but without the meat, tightly seal the container with a lid, and shake vigorously to mix.

Add the meat to the container mix, and again shake vigorously for several minutes, to get the liquid mixture to coat all of the meat pieces.

Chill overnight if possible to marinate, and flip the container over 3 or 4 times in that period to keep the liquid moving through the meat pieces.

Remove the container from the refrigerator, and using a large sauce pan, pour the entire contents into the pan set on medium high heat. Brown and braise uncovered for about 3 minutes on each side, allowing some of the sugar mixture to caramelize and adhere to the meat. The inside of the meat pieces and some edges should still be red and not totally cooked at this stage.

Add the butter, scallions, and mushrooms, as shown in picture **B**. Brown on medium heat, uncovered, for another 6 minutes.

Add Worcestershire sauce and one full bottle of beer. I have used a strong Blue Moon Belgian ale, since it is my favorite and in the refrigerator, but any strong beer will do including dark beers which many cooks prefer in this type of recipe. Cook uncovered for 6 minutes allowing some liquid to evaporate.

Cover and simmer for another 10 minutes

Prepare the pasta of your choice. I recommend egg noodles, as are traditionally served with beef tips.

Place a portion of noodles on serving plate, and ladle the beef tips and broth/gravy onto the center of the pasta, and serve while hot. Serving shown in picture **C**.

A

B

C

Be sure of the hill you want to die on. Is it worth the price. Pick your battles wisely.

40

Rib Roast

Danita's Delight

Ingredients

1 rib eye roast bone-in (3 to 4 lbs.)

Seasoning

Ketchup

Honey Dijon mustard

Olive oil

Minced garlic

Each pound of meat is one serving

A Bone from Pennie

If you mess this one up KNUCKLEHEAD, someone needs to slap you right across that snot locker of yours hanging on the front of your face. This is an expensive cut of meat and deserves your full attention.

If desired, cut small slits in the meat surfaces of the roast, and insert slices of fresh garlic.

This dish will make a mess of the pot if not lined with aluminum foil. The high temperatures tend to burn a non-stick spray like PAM so I recommend the foil for this particular recipe.

The main function of the ketchup coating is to hold the moisture of the meat inside the roast, and to hold some spice and flavor to the two end cuts. It will get dark brown or even blacken. If the coating does over cook, then lightly scrape it off the roast, trying to leave some of the spice on the meat.

Directions

Pre-heat oven to 550 degrees (broil setting). Hand rub the meat with olive oil to coat all surfaces. Lightly rub a small amount of dry spice mix or meat seasoning onto the meat surfaces of the roast. It is not necessary to add any spice to the bone side. The rib eye roast is shown in picture **A** with the ingredients and Dutch oven for baking.

In a small bowl, add 1/2 cup of ketchup, 2 TBSP of honey Dijon mustard, 2 TBSP minced garlic, 1 TBSP garlic salt, and 3 TBSP dry meat seasoning, and mix.

Using a spoon, generously coat all of the meat surfaces with the liquid mix. The picture on the left side of picture **B** shows the roast with a scoop of the ketchup sauce mix placed on top of the roast. The right hand picture shows the roast fully covered with the sauce and then coated with bread crumbs. The bread crumbs are optional but do help hold the ketchup sauce in place on the sides of the roast. Use your hands if you need to, but make sure the top and sides of the meat are well covered. I use rib eyes for almost all of my meat entrée's, as a personal choice, but porterhouse, and T-bone cuts are perfect for this type of pan frying as well.

Place roast, bone-side down, in a tightly sealed Dutch oven, or seal tightly with aluminum foil, and place in the pre-heated oven for 45 minutes, and set the timer. When the timer sounds, turn the heat OFF, but do not open the oven door, allowing the roast to continue to bake as the heat slowly lessens in the closed oven, for an additional 60 minutes. Set your timer.

When the timer sounds, the roast is cooked. Remove from the oven with mitts or pot holders, and place on stove top or proper hot mat. Remove the roast and place on plate to serve while hot, as shown in picture **C**. Slices will be the width of the bottom rib bone, or about 1-inch thick. The two end cuts are spicier and more well done than the center cut pieces.

When you teach someone the lesson of meanness, don't be surprised if they learn.

Chicken & Sausage Shake and Bake

Hello Nawlins

Ingredients

4 skinless chicken breasts.

4 Italian sausage links

1 small can of mandarin oranges

1/2 cup sliced onions

1/2 cup olive oil

2 TBSP honey Dijon mustard

1 TBSP Worcestershire sauce

1 TBSP fresh chopped sage

1 TBSP ground pepper

1/2 TBSP salt

Serves 4

A Bone from Pennie

Scared to try this recipe? Come on KNUCKLEHEAD, show a little brass between those walking sticks and go for it.

If you do not have a one gallon double sealing plastic storage bag to use for marinating the chicken, use a large mixing bowl with well sealing lid, which will work just as well.

The longer the chicken stays in the marinade the more flavor it absorbs. If you want to prepare the chicken early in the morning, and refrigerate for about 10 or 12 hours until dinner time, that will work. However, overnight works the best.

Be light with the seasoning you add on the chicken in the pan. The marinade has already put a lot of flavoring and seasoning into the chicken.

I find this to be the most aromatic dish of all the recipes. Get ready for your house to smell wonderful.

Directions

Using a one gallon double sealing storage plastic bag, add the can of mandarin oranges with juice, seal the bag, and carefully massage and squeeze the orange slices to break them up into smaller pieces.

Add all other ingredients, except for meat, and gently shake and mix thoroughly.

Add the chicken only to the liquid, seal the plastic bag, and shake to coat the chicken pieces with the liquid mix. Chill overnight in the refrigerator, as the chicken marinates. Try to flip the container over from time to time to keep the liquid marinade continually covering the chicken pieces, as shown in picture **A**.

Remove the chicken and marinade container from the refrigerator, and allow the chicken to sit at room temperature for about 30 to 45 minutes.

Pre-heat oven to 400 degrees.

Using an oven safe dish, place the chicken pieces and all of the marinade liquid into the dish, and season lightly with all purpose seasoning, or seasoning of your choice.

Add sausages interspersed evenly throughout the pan, as shown in picture **B** (shown before baking). Do not cover.

Set timer, and bake for 30 minutes. Remove the dish from the oven, and flip both the sausages and the chicken, and place back in the oven to bake an additional 30 minutes, or until both the chicken and sausage are browned on the outside, and no pink remains on the inside of the chicken pieces.

Picture **C** shows the completed dish. Notice that about half of the liquid has cooked out of the mix leaving the dark brown mark around the dish above the food. This is normal and desired for this dish.

Serve one breast and one sausage as a serving.

There are several theories to arguing with women. None of them work.

Country Chicken

Ballay's Binge

Ingredients

7 to 10 chicken thighs

Seasoning

3 TBSP oil

Note: This is a two part recipe, wherein we will serve 2 to 4 thighs as an entrée from the recipe on this page, and the rest of the thighs, after cooking, will be leftover and used for the next recipe on page 44 to the right. If served strictly as an entree then 2 thighs make one serving.

Serves 2

A Bone from Pennie

This recipe is so easy KNUCKLeHead, that if you screw it up, you may want to think about taking yourself out of the gene pool.

You can use any type of chicken pieces whether thighs, wings, drumsticks, breasts , etc. Breasts can become a bit dry if even slightly overcooked though, so be careful. You may also use pieces with the skin on, or skinless. Either is okay.

For the purposes of making the next dish, make up 2 full cups of dry rice. Use up to 2 cups of cooked rice for the side dish and save the rest for later, approximately 4 cups.

When adding wet meat to a hot pan with oil, be careful not to splash yourself with hot oil, and watch out for the oil "popping" and getting on your arms and hands as well.

When 4 thighs are removed for this entrée, you should have 3 to 5 thighs left in the pan with about 1 to 2 cups of liquid. Set aside to cool for now.

Directions

You probably cannot find an entrée recipe that has fewer ingredients than we have here, and shown in picture **A**. This is *comfort food* at its finest, and this dish is a standby favorite in my house.

Take the chicken thighs and wash them in cold water, place them on a paper towel and dab dry with an additional paper towel.

Pour 3 TBSP of oil in a large saucepan that can accommodate 7 to 10 pieces of chicken.

Season one side to taste, and place the thighs in the large saucepan that has a good sealing lid for later, making sure to put the season side down. Fill up the sauce pan as much as possible (picture **B**). Season the top side of the pieces while in the pan, and the seasoned side down is browning. Cook on medium to medium high heat for 10 to 15 minutes, flipping the pieces every 3 to 4 minutes to lightly brown and crisp up both sides. DO NOT totally cook the chicken pieces at this stage, just get the outside a little crispy with a light golden brown color.

Turn the heat down to low, and add about 3 cups of water, or until the water comes up about 2/3 to 3/4 of the way on the thighs. Do not cover the top of the thighs with water. Cover the dish with the lid, and set your timer for 60 minutes. You should see a slow bubbling boil around the chicken pieces. Periodically check the dish and make sure the water level does not get much below half way down on the chicken pieces.

Prepare either rice or mashed potatoes as a side.

Use a large spoon to remove 1/2 cup of the liquid from the pan, after completion of cooking time, placing it in a measuring cup and adding 1 TBSP of corn starch (or 2 TBSP of flour), stirring continually and rapidly to make a gravy. Serve as shown in picture **C**.

A

B

C

You can learn by reading, observation, listening, or hard knocks. The first three are much easier.

Country Fried Rice

Hoot's Own

Ingredients

4 cups leftover rice

3 to 5 leftover chicken thighs

1 to 1-1/2 cups leftover liquid

3 scrambled eggs (no milk added)

1 cup frozen corn

1 cup frozen peas

1 cup frozen carrots

2 TBSP soy sauce

Serves 4 to 6

A Bone from Pennie

Let me get this straight KNUCKLeHead; Out of 400,000 sperm, you were the fastest? Unbelievable.

You can use fresh vegetables in lieu of the frozen specified, but frozen vegetables tend to hold their texture and shape much better in this dish.

You can add any other vegetables you may prefer, such as mushrooms or bamboo sprouts, etc. Whatever you substitute though, make sure you get those items properly cooked.

There is a lot of leftover seasoning in the liquid from the first dish on page 43, and soy sauce has flavor and sodium in it, so very little additional seasoning is required. Season to taste while the dish is cooking.

This dish can be refrigerated for 3 to 4 days easily. When reheating in a microwave add a little bit of water over the rice before heating to help moisturize the rice, and other ingredients.

Directions

Take the leftover thighs from the previous dish on page 43, which should be cool to the touch before handling, 3 to 5 pieces being required, and remove them to a plate or cutting board. Shred the chicken by hand, as seen in picture **A** along with the other ingredients. Tear the meat into large bite size pieces, and discard the bones.

Return the sauce pan containing the liquid and leftover chicken chunks and seasoning to the stove top burner. Make sure you have not, or do not, try and clean out the pan, as we will be using the seasoning and liquid form the previous dish. Add water if necessary to get at least 1-1/2 cups of liquid, and reheat to a slow boil on medium heat, gently scraping the bottom with a wooden spoon, to loosen up anything left clinging to the bottom of the pan . It is not necessary for you to measure the liquid, but try and get as close to the proper amount as you can visually assess.

Add the soy sauce and let cook for 2 to 3 minutes. Place all ingredients into the pan and the heated liquids, as shown in picture **B**, and leaving the dish uncovered, cook on medium heat, stirring occasionally, until most of the liquid is either dispersed or absorbed by the ingredients.

With the large amount of meat in this dish, it is easily served as a stand alone entrée as shown in picture **C**. However it can also be served as a side dish to other entrée's as well.

Life can be taken from you or those you love at any moment. Carpe Diem.

44

Baked BBQ Ribs

Mizzou Mania

Ingredients

Country style ribs (2 to 3 pounds)

1 bottle of barbecue sauce

Ketchup

Mustard

2 TBSP vinegar

4 TBSP brown sugar

1/4 cup chopped onions

Serves 4

Note: This is a two part recipe; the leftovers will be used to prepare the pulled pork dish in the next recipe, on page 46. If you desire to have leftovers to use for the pulled pork dish, then be sure and cook a large amount of ribs in this recipe.

A Bone from Pennie

Lord grant us the inner strength not to squeeze the fois gras out of this KNUCKLeHead, who so richly deserves it. Speaking of squeezing, do not go nuts with the ketchup bottle, just because I told you that you did not have to specifically measure the amount. Less is better.

Do not over season the ribs, as the other ingredients contain a lot of seasoning and flavoring.

Be sure to use enough aluminum foil to get a good seal, to keep the moisture in. If you have a covered oven dish, then that will suffice, and the aluminum foil is not necessary.

If you plan on placing the baking dish on the table, for everyone to serve themselves, then I suggest you lightly stir the liquid ingredients, as it will make a more attractive plating appearance.

Make this one correct and it will be one giant step for morons; one giant leap for KNUCKLeHeadS.

Directions

Pre-heat oven to 500 degrees

Choose an oven safe dish that will hold all the ribs somewhat snuggly, without layering or overlapping the ribs. Lightly coat the ribs with olive oil and place in the bottom of the dish. Season the ribs to taste with dry spice rub or salt and pepper as you prefer, as shown in picture **A**.

Pour the bottle of barbecue sauce onto the ribs. Fill the barbecue sauce bottle up half way with clean water, add the vinegar to the mix, place the lid back on the bottle, shake well, and pour water and remaining sauce mix onto the ribs.

Take the ketchup bottle and add about one cup of ketchup. It is not necessary to precisely measure the ketchup, so you may squirt the ketchup directly into the mix.

Repeat this procedure with the mustard, adding approximately 2 TBSP of yellow mustard.

Evenly distribute the onions into the mix.

Sprinkle the brown sugar on top. At this point your ribs and sauce should look like the dish in picture **B**. You may very gently stir the sauce to mix the ingredients, being sure not to disturb the ribs by stirring only the top sauce portion, or you may leave it exactly as it appears in picture **B**, which will leave a sweet crust on top when complete.

Cover tightly with aluminum foil, and place in the oven for 45 minutes. Set the timer.

When the timer sounds, turn the oven OFF, without opening the oven, and allow the dish to cook for an additional 45 minutes in the closed oven. Set the timer again, and when it goes off the dish is cooked. Remove from the oven with mitts or pot holders. Dish will appear as seen in picture **C**. Serve on plate with scoops of sauce. Cover and store leftover ribs and sauce in same baking dish.

A

B

C

Few men lie on their death beds and wish they had worked more. Smell the roses along life's journey.

Pulled Pork

Mizzou DQ

Ingredients

Leftover baked BBQ ribs and sauce from the previous recipe on page 45 to the left.

One leftover rib will make sufficient pulled pork for one large sandwich

A Bone from Pennie

You are standing there KNUCKLEHEAD, looking as uncomfortable and nervous as a prostitute in church. Relax, follow the directions and you'll be fine. It is leftovers after all.

You do not have to store the leftovers in the same dish they were cooked in, but I find that easiest, and one less bowl to clean later.

The cold pork ribs can be a little difficult sometimes to break up into small pieces. You may find it easier to bake them for 10 or 15 minutes, remove the bowl from the oven, and continue breaking and shredding the pieces by using a fork, before placing back in the oven to continue warming and baking.

If you choose, you may also reheat the pork in a large sauce pan on the stove top in lieu of the oven, and heat for the same amount of time with a temperature setting of medium.

Add brown sugar for additional sweetness if desired.

Directions

Pre-heat oven to 350 degrees.

Hopefully you kept the leftover baked barbecue ribs and sauce from the previous recipe, and covered them and kept them in the refrigerator overnight. Retrieve the ribs in the baking dish from the refrigerator, uncover, and place the cold dish on a working surface.

You will find that the fat and oil has coagulated on the surface of the sauce as a hard orange substance, as shown in picture **A**. This can be removed with a spoon, as I am doing in the picture. Discard the substance in the trash, and not in your garbage disposal.

Pull all the ribs out of the sauce and place on a cutting board. Using your hands pull the pork ribs into small pieces. Picture **B** shows 4 leftover ribs that I have torn into bite size pieces, alongside the original baking dish which still contains the leftover sauce. I prefer the larger pieces as shown, but many people prefer to have the pork pulled and shredded into even smaller pieces. Either is fine.

Place all of the pulled pork pieces back into the dish with the sauce. Leave the dish uncovered and place into the pre-heated oven for 30 minutes.

Remove the dish carefully, using oven mitts or pot holders, and place on stove top, and stir.

You may serve the barbecue pulled pork as a sandwich, as I have shown in picture **C**, or serve on top of any type of bread as an open face sandwich. I sometimes serve this dish over rice or noodles as well.

Place leftover pulled pork and sauce in a sealed container, and store for up to 4 days.

When reheating, remove and heat only the portions you plan to eat; not the entire leftover container.

A

B

C

If the enemy is in range, then so are you.

Hamburger Steak

Randy's Right

Ingredients

1 pound of ground meat

Seasoning

Mushrooms (optional)

Onion (optional)

Oil

One pound of raw ground meat makes 2 servings. You may cook as many patties as desired, and of the size you prefer.

A Bone from Pennie

You are so oblivious to things you KNUCKLEHEAD. I do believe the entire Prussian army could march through your kitchen, and you would never pick up on it. Follow the recipe!

If you like the inside of the hamburger steak pink, try making the steaks a little thicker, but do not go much thicker than 3/4-inch or you will see red instead of pink.

You can be a little creative, and add any of the things you like in the meat before cooking such as green bell pepper pieces, jalapeno peppers, shredded cheese, olives, etc.

Hamburger steaks are traditionally served with the sautéed mushrooms on top. If you want a gravy mix for the top garnish, then remove the patties from the saucepan when they are cooked and place to the side. Mix 2 TBSP of corn starch in 1/4 cup of warm water, stir well, and pour into the warm pan. Use a flat-end wooden spoon and deglaze the bottom of the pan and cook gravy for 1 to 2 minutes on medium heat.

Directions

Place the ground meat onto a cutting board, and spread out the meat. Mince 1/4 cup of red onion, and add it to the ground meat (onion is optional- individual preference).

Season the ground meat with garlic salt and pepper, and some all purpose seasoning of your choice, as shown in picture **A**. Using your hands, knead the ground meat together and evenly blend the seasonings and onions into the ground meat mix.

Form patties to the size you desire. Ground meat will tend to shrink a little while cooking, so make the raw patties slightly wider than you wish to have when completed cooking.

Make the patties about 1/2 inch thick, and the center of the patty should be slightly concave, and not mounded or rounded up. As the meat cooks, and the paddy shrinks inward, the center of the patty will rise upward a little to make a flat hamburger steak when complete.

Using a large flat bottom sauce pan as shown in picture **B**, add 2 TBSP of cooking oil, and cook the patties for 6 to 8 minutes on medium high heat. If you like the hamburger steaks medium, leave the pan uncovered while you cook. If however you desire the steaks to be well done then cover the pan while you are cooking the steaks. Cook each side for about 2 minutes, then flip the patties and repeat. Do not overcook the patties. Each side should be cooked twice for two minutes each, or a total cooking time of 8 minutes, depending on how thick the patties are, whether you want rare or well done, and the size pan and temperature setting you use. Use common sense as you cook, but overcooking may make the hamburger steaks tough.

In a separate small sauce pan, braise some mushrooms in 2 TBSP of butter for 4 minutes on medium high, and add on top of the hamburger steaks, as shown in picture **C**.

When you are searching for answers or motives, you need only follow the money trail.

47

Beef Stew

Mountain Grove

Ingredients

2 pounds boneless beef stew meat

3 TBSP olive oil

3 TBSP flour

1 large red onion diced

2 TBSP minced garlic

2 bay leaves

1 TSP thyme

1 cup bold red wine (cabernet)

1 cup carrots

1 cup small new or red potatoes

1/2 cup frozen green peas

1/2 cup frozen corn

2 TBSP parsley

Serves 6 to 8

A Bone from Pennie

Are you singing KNUCKLEHEAD, or did your pet elk accidentally rupture himself? Tell him this is beef stew and not elk stew, so not to worry.

The key to this entire recipe is keeping the meat tender and juicy, and not letting it dry out. The way we do that is using a heavy-based pot with a tight fitting lid, like the cast iron Dutch oven shown.

If you like the vegetables a little firmer, then add them at the half way point (30 minutes) of the final baking phase.

Don't be afraid to add a little oil in the first cooking phases, to keep the mix liquid and preventing burning. The same is true for baking, when you may need to add some water if the stew becomes to dry or starts to scorch.

If you like turnips, you may add them with the potatoes, but not before the half way point of baking time.

Directions

Pre-heat oven to 400 degrees.

Prepare meat in bite sized pieces, and season to taste. Reference picture **A** for size of pieces.

In a large sauce pan, with heat set at medium high, add olive oil, allowing it come up to temperature, then add the seasoned meat to brown. Sear the meat, stirring occasionally, until the meat has a dark brown crusty surface. Do not burn. This step should take about 10 to 12 minutes.

Remove the meat using a slotted spoon, to a plate on the side (right side picture **A**), leaving the remaining oil and liquid in the pan. Lower temperature to medium, and add the onions, garlic, thyme, and bay leaves, stirring frequently, and cook for 5 minutes, until onions are soft. Add another TBSP of oil if the mix becomes too dry.

Pour 1 cup of red wine, and 2 cups of water into the pan, add the flour, and stir. Cook for 5 minutes (left side picture **A**). Add the beef to the liquid, and cook an additional 5 minutes. Add potatoes, peas, corn, and carrots and stir softly, making sure not to break up the ingredients, as shown in picture **B**. Cook for 3 minutes.

Pour the entire hot mix into a Dutch oven or cast iron utensil that has a good sealing lid. Use a very large piece of foil that extends about 4 to 6 inches past all edges, and covers the top rim, then gently push down the center of the foil, as shown in picture **C**, but not quite touching the stew. Use two pieces of foil if necessary, cross lapping them, to get a good coverage and seal. Tightly crimp the foil edges around the rim and cover with lid.

Place the pot in the pre-heated oven for 75 minutes, being sure to set a timer. Discard bay leaves and serve. Dish can be served on its own, or over pasta or rice.

A

B

C

There is no such thing as a secret. Bank on it.

Shrimp Scampi

Holland's Hit

Ingredients

2 pounds frozen cooked shrimp

1 1/2 sticks of real butter

Garlic

Seasoning

Serves 2

A Bone from Pennie

Call your doctor **KNUCKLEHEAD**, and tell him you want your money back; the lobotomy didn't take. At least that should be your position if you mess this one up.

The choice of shrimp is really the only variable in this dish. The shrimp I have chosen to use are frozen, deveined, cooked, tail-on shrimp that have a "count" of 21 to 25 pieces per pound. All of this information is available on the front of the frozen shrimp packaging. Frozen shrimp are less expensive and more readily available than fresh shrimp.

If you decide to use fresh shrimp, then you will need to peel the shrimp, including removal of the tails, and de-vein the shrimp by slicing down the back of the shrimp and removing the dark gray vein located in the back of each separate shrimp. Fresh shrimp will also require more time to cook in the sauce, usually about 6 to 8 minutes on medium heat, while continually stirring the shrimp and sauce.

Directions

Remove tails, black back vein, and peels (depending on what type of frozen shrimp you purchase), and set to the side, as shown in picture **A**.

Prepare two servings of pasta (page 10). While your pasta is cooking, continue with the shrimp scampi preparation.

Using a large sauce pan, set it on the stove top and turn the heat to low or medium low. Place the butter in the pan to slowly melt. Do not allow the butter to over heat or boil. Add some minced garlic, 2 TBSP is sufficient, or add thin slices of fresh garlic if desired. Lightly season the sauce with salt, pepper, or any type of general purpose seasoning.

Allow all of the butter to melt, forming a rich golden yellow sauce as shown in picture **B**, and heat the sauce for one minute, keeping the heat on low.

Place the thawed cooked shrimp into the warm butter sauce, and turn the heat up to medium. Since the shrimp are already *cooked*, you need only warm the meat of the shrimp up to a nice warm temperature, which will take about 2 to 3 minutes, but no more than that amount. Over cooking the shrimp or over heating them in this stage will cause them to get hard and tough. The sauce should just start to bubble, coming to a light boil, at which time you should be complete. If the shrimp are not hot, then continue to heat for a minute or so.

The completed dish is shown in picture **C**, without the shrimp scampi on the pasta, so that you can better visualize how the completed scampi dish should appear before serving it onto the pasta.

A

B

C

Listen to yourself, know yourself, believe in yourself, and trust yourself.

London Broil Steak

Crisp's Choice

Ingredients

1 to 2 pound London Broil steak

Olive oil

Butter

Seasoning to taste

*****

Topping:

1 cup mushrooms

1/2 cup diced red onion

1/4 cup butter

Season to taste

Serves 3 to 4

A Bone from Pennie

That dizzy sensation you are feeling, KNUCKLEHEAD, is because you are circling the drain. There may not be much hope for you, but we can keep you from being hungry as you go down.

London broil is a much less expensive cut of meat, than for instance the rib eyes that I use so often. Don't let that bother you, as once it is properly prepared, as with this recipe, it will taste just as good as the expensive cuts.

It is *imperative* that you cut the slices about 1/4 to 3/8 inch thick and across the grain, as shown. If you do not cut across the grain, the small grains of meat will be string like and tough.

I love to turn this into a barbecue dish. Once complete per recipe, lightly coat with barbecue sauce, broil for 3 minutes, slice as described and cover with warm barbecue sauce of your choice. Delicious!

Directions

This is a two part recipe; first the preparation of the meat, and secondly the topping.

Place the cut of London Broil meat on a cutting board, and coat generously with olive oil. Using a standard fork, pierce the meat about one hundred times or so, to tenderize. Picture **A** shows the marks from the fork tines, and gives you an idea of the frequency and spacing of the piercing.

Flip the cut of meat over and repeat the piercing for the other side as well. Season both sides to taste, with salt and pepper or an all purpose seasoning. Set meat aside to rest while you prepare the topping.

Melt butter in small sauce pan on medium heat. When the butter is almost totally melted, add mushrooms and onions, as shown in picture **B**, season to taste, and cook on medium heat for 6 to 8 minutes, stirring frequently, until onions are soft, and mushrooms are brown. Turn heat down to simmer and monitor while the London Broil steak is prepared. Keep warm until steak is complete.

Using a large flat bottom sauce pan, melt about 1/2 stick of butter on medium heat. Do not boil or burn the butter.

Add the prepared piece of London Broil, turn heat up to medium high, and cook each side one time for about 6 to 7 minutes on each side. Remove the steak onto a cutting board, and *slice across the grain* of the meat, cutting sections about 1/4 inch thick. Picture **C** shows a serving of meat, topping on the side, along with mashed potatoes.

A

B

C

Always buy good shoes and a good mattress. You'll understand why later on in life.

Garlic Shrimp

Craig's Crunchies

Ingredients

1 pound cleaned shrimp in shell

Seasoning

1/3 cup minced garlic with juice

Olive oil (spray is optional)

Serves 2

A Bone from Pennie

Have you ever wondered KNUCKLEHEAD why your mother cries every time she sees you. Well I'm starting to get a grasp on that one, as I watch you battle these shrimp.

Over seasoning is a common error on this dish. Go light with the seasoning, as you can always add some later if desired.

If you over cook the shrimp under the broiler, it will get tough or hard to chew. The precise location in regards to the broiler in the top of the oven, will vary the cooking time on the shrimp. Error on the side of caution, and check the shrimp at 2 to 3 minutes for completion, and place the dish back under the broiler if necessary.

Be sure and add the garlic juices from the minced garlic, onto the shrimp. The liquid will permeate the meat and add flavor.

Serve immediately from the oven.

Directions

Collect and prepare the basic ingredients as shown in picture **A**.

Make sure the shrimp are clean, vein removed, filleted open, and remain in shell. Rinse shrimp thoroughly.

Select a large baking dish, and spray with non stick Pam.

Place the shrimp, shell side down/meat side up, in the baking dish.

Spray the shrimp with olive oil, or generously drizzle olive oil in a bottle over all of the shrimp.

Season to taste. Do not over season, as the shrimp have a strong succulent flavor on their own, and you don't want to overpower the natural taste.

Spread minced garlic over all of the shrimp, until you have a dish that appears as shown in picture **B**. (This is a very heavy application of garlic. When first trying this dish you may want to use less garlic, until you achieve the desired level for your personal taste).

Allow the seasoned shrimp to rest for 10 minutes, to marinate, before proceeding, as you pre-heat the oven to 550 degrees/broil setting.

Place the baking dish uncovered in the middle or towards the top of the oven, but not on the very top rack next to the broiler itself. Broil for 3 to 4 minutes, or until shrimp is cooked to a white meat.

Using oven mitts, remove the dish from the oven and set on protected surface. The dish is complete and should look like the one shown in picture **C**.

Use tongs to place the shrimp on dinner plates, and serve while hot. Provide melted butter for dipping if desired, and an extra saucer for shells.

A

B

C

Others may be stronger or smarter, so don't let them outwork you.

51

KNUCKLEHEAD NOTES:

Side Dishes For a Knucklehead

Bachelor, New Graduate, Beginner, and other Knuckleheads

Side dishes are meant to compliment the main course, and to provide balance to your diet. For this reason, I have chosen to include some very basic day-to-day recipes for such things as green beans, peas, corn, mashed potatoes, etc., and a couple of more exotic side dish recipes as well.

Most people prefer the taste of fresh vegetables over canned vegetables when possible. I have included and shown these recipes using a lot of canned vegetables and produce, since they are usually more readily available. You can always substitute fresh vegetables for the canned version. Go easy with your seasonings, and let the flavor of the produce carry these side dishes, and whatever you do, don't miss the red beans and rice recipe.

Baked Potato

Debbie's Favorite

Ingredients

Large Idaho potatoes

Corn oil

Sea Salt

One large potato is one serving

A Bone from Pennie

So simple, even a KNUCKLeHead can fix this one.

I promise you these baked potatoes are wonderfully perfect. A lot of the vitamins in a potato are located in and around the skin. By preparing the outside of the potato skin with the sea salt, allows the healthy skin of the potato to become part of the dish, and not just a holding vessel.

Everyone loves to prepare potatoes in a different manner. My favorite is butter and bacon bits. A dollop of sour cream is a traditional topping as well. You can also prepare a few small dishes of various toppings such as finely chopped shallots, anchovies, chives, butter, bacon bits, etc., and serve a tray of toppings so everyone can fix their own potato in their favorite manner.

Potatoes vary a lot in size, and therefore will cook in different amounts of time. Remove one potato and check with fork for tenderness, and return to oven if necessary.

Directions

Pre-heat oven to 550 degrees/broil.

Arrange all ingredients shown in picture **A** on a clean work surface.

Tear off one large piece of aluminum foil for each individual potato. Don't be skimpy with the foil, as the larger pieces will prevent the oil from dripping out.

Pour corn oil into the palm of one hand, then place potato in same palm, rubbing the oil over the entire surface of the potato. Sprinkle salt onto the potato and place an oiled and salted potato on each piece of foil.

Referencing picture **B**:

* Top left; place potato diagonally on foil.

* Top right; Wrap corner of foil over top of potato.

* Bottom left; Wrap two side corners on potato.

* Bottom right; Roll potato towards remaining corner and tightly seal foil onto the potato.

Place tightly wrapped and sealed potatoes in the pre-heated oven, and set the timer for 60 minutes.

When the timer sounds, turn off the heat, and reset the timer for 30 minutes, and let the potatoes continue to cook as the temperature gradually dissipates.

When the timer sounds the second time (1 hour 30 minutes total cooking time) the potatoes are done.

Using oven mitts, remove the potatoes and unwrap from foil. Picture **C** shows a properly baked and salted potato on bottom left, and a prepared and buttered baked potato on the upper right. The meat of the potato will still need some salt.

A

B

C

Hold on. Hold fast. Hold tight. Patience usually pays off.

Potato Salad

Sophie's Choice

Ingredients

3 cups diced red potatoes

3 boiled eggs

3 small sweet peppers

1 cup Miracle Whip

1/2 cup mustard

3 sliced shallots

3 TBSP sweet relish

3 TBSP all purpose flour

3 TBSP sugar

3 TBSP vinegar

1 TBSP parsley flakes

1 TSP paprika

1 TSP salt

1 TSP ground black pepper

Serves 6

A Bone from Pennie

Sometimes KNUCKLeHeaD, you seem to be as blind as a bridegroom. Read and follow the directions, and you can handle this somewhat involved recipe.

You will need 4 medium sized red potatoes to make the three cups of chopped potatoes specified in the ingredient list. Accordingly it would take about 3 large potatoes or 6 small red potatoes.

Leave the skins on the potatoes. So many of the good vitamins are in the skin or upper surface, and the red coloring adds to the appearance of the dish.

Brown potatoes work fine as well, but you may want to peel them first, as the brown skins seem to give the dish a little bit of a dirty appearance.

Substitute dill relish for the sweet, and/or mayonnaise for the Miracle Whip if you desire a less sweet potato salad.

Directions

Wash the red potatoes and cut into cubes about the size of game dice (reference picture **A**). Place the potatoes in a cooking pot with water, bring the water to a boil, and cook the potatoes for 20 minutes. Set the timer.

While the potatoes are boiling, peel the boiled eggs, double slice in egg slicer, and put them in a large mixing bowl.

Thinly slice the celery, peppers, and shallots and place those in the mixing bowl with the eggs.

Place a colander in the bottom of the kitchen sink, carefully remove the pot of boiling potatoes, and pour the water and potatoes into the colander, as shown in picture **B**. Add the potatoes into the mixing bowl, and sprinkle the salt, pepper, parsley flakes, and paprika directly onto the potatoes.

Add all other ingredients into the bowl. Using a wooden spoon or spatula, gently fold the ingredients together for several minutes, until all of the ingredients are uniformly mixed.

Potato Salad is best served cold, directly from the refrigerator. Refrigerate in a covered container for a minimum of 2 hours. You may leave the potato salad in the bowl, covered, and store in the refrigerator for up to three days with no ill effects.

Picture **C** shows a serving of the potato salad in a salad bowl, which was done for presentation purposes only. Potato salad is more commonly served as a side dish on the plate with the main entrée, such as barbecue ribs. You may wish to serve it on a bed of lettuce for plating appearance.

Any type of mustard can be used. Traditional potato salad uses a plain yellow mustard. In this picture you will see that I have used a coarse ground Dijon mustard, which adds a lot of *zip* to the dish, and more of a brown coloring, in lieu of normal yellow.

A

B

C

Life is not fair and holds no guarantees. When you lose, don't forget the lesson.

Mashed Potatoes

Panther Passion

Ingredients

4 cups sliced and peeled potatoes

1 cup milk

1/2 cup butter

1 TBSP olive oil

3 TBSP minced garlic with juice

1 TSP salt

1/2 TSP pepper

Serves 8

A Bone from Pennie

We can put a man on the moon, erect buildings a half mile high, and create computers faster and smarter than Einstein, but KNUCKLEHEAD, teaching you to cook may be man's greatest challenge.

Do not over cook the potatoes. Check them at about 15 minutes of boiling, and if they are soft throughout, then they are done and you can proceed to the next stage. The smaller or thinner the potato slices, the faster they will cook.

Do not overbeat the potatoes. When they get fluffy, stop. Otherwise you will get a milky substance that only resembles mashed potatoes.

If you are in a hurry, cut the potatoes into small cubes about the size of dice. Boiling will only take about 8 to 10 minutes.

Garnish with fresh parsley if desired.

Reference page 57 for leftover recipe.

Directions

Cut and peel potatoes, and rinse thoroughly.

Cut the potatoes into circular segments, no more than one inch thick, as shown in picture **A**.

Place potatoes into a large sauce pan, add water to completely cover potatoes, and set temperature to medium high, and wait for water to boil.

When water begins to boil, set the timer for 20 minutes, and let the potatoes boil the entire time.

While potatoes are boiling, place butter and garlic into a microwave safe container, and heat until butter starts to melt or is very soft.

Pour potatoes and water into a colander set in the bottom of the sink, and let drain. Do not rinse.

Transfer potatoes to a large mixing bowl, while still hot, and add rest of ingredients, as shown in picture **B**.

Use an electric mixer, and beat the potato mix at medium speed, until all ingredients are uniformly mixed, and the potatoes are fluffy.

The mashed potatoes are now complete and ready to be served.

Picture **C** shows a scoop of mashed potatoes on a serving plate, with a concave "pond" in the potatoes, in which I have placed a pad of butter. You can also place gravies or drippings into the hollow of the mashed potatoes as well.

Serve while hot.

A

B

C

Honor this nation, the men and women who defend her, and those who died in her defense. Despite any problems it is the greatest nation on earth.

56

Potato Patties

Broyle's Brew

Ingredients

1.5 cups leftover mashed potatoes

1 egg

1/4 cup finely chopped onion

2 TBSP finely chopped sweet pepper

1/4 TSP baking powder

1/4 cup flour

Serves 4 (4 patties)

A Bone from Pennie

Lord grant me patience to deal with this KNUCKLEHEAD, and I want it right now. I think I have more hope for a bobble-head to succeed with this recipe, than I have for you to pull it off, but come on; lets give it a whirl.

Remember that leftover mashed potatoes are already seasoned.

I prefer not to use very creamy mashed potatoes, but rather to leave some small potato chunks in the mix. Either one is okay, but if you are making the potatoes fresh for this recipe, then try and leave some chunks and lumps in the mix.

The mashed potatoes are already cooked, so it is not necessary to overcook these patties. Cook only once on each side.

This recipe is an old Midwest classic from my mom. They are great with fried fish or fried chicken. The potato patties will compliment almost any meat dish.

Directions

If you have leftover mashed potatoes, you may use them, or you may make the mashed potatoes from scratch, using the recipe on page 56. You will need approximately 1-1/2 cups of mashed potatoes, and the other ingredients shown in picture **A**.

Place the mashed potatoes in a medium size mixing bowl.

Prepare 1/4 cup finely chopped onion.

(Optional: Prepare 2 TBSP finely chopped sweet peppers).

Place all ingredients in the bowl, and mix thoroughly with a mixer on low speed.

Depending on how wet or dry your mashed potatoes are, it may be necessary to add some more flour to thicken the mix, but it should not take much, if any.

Using a large flat bottom sauce pan, add 2 Tbsp of vegetable oil, set the heat for medium, and allow the oil to get hot.

Using a large spoon, place four equal amounts of potato batter in the pan, as shown in picture **B**, cook for 2 minutes (or until golden brown), flip over with turner, and repeat for the other side.

If the mix is very thick in consistency, it may be necessary, after the first flip, to use the flat bottom of the turner to slightly mash down the patties, so that they are no more than 1/2 inch thick in the middle.

Picture **C** shows 4 patties that have been cooked, and placed on a serving platter.

Serve while the patties are hot or warm. Excellent side dish for red beans and rice entrée. This is true comfort food.

A

B

C

Respect and take care of the elderly. Hopefully you will be there as well one day.

57

Garlic Green Beans

Abbie's Add On

Ingredients

16 ounce can of green beans

3 TBSP butter

2 chopped shallots

1 TBSP minced garlic with juice

Season to taste

Serves 4

A Bone from Pennie

Don't overcook the green beans KNUCKLEHEAD, or they will taste like they've been strained through dirty socks.

This dish is even better when using fresh green beans. Buy one pound of fresh beans, wash, remove string on the seam of the beans, and rinse, before proceeding with the dish.

These beans need to be crisp and somewhat firm. Do not over cook the beans in the first step.

Finely chopped onion is acceptable substitute for the shallots.

Don't let the butter scorch and burn, or it will ruin the taste of the entire dish.

I seasoned this dish with a little salt and fresh ground peppercorns. An all purpose seasoning or vegetable seasoning is very good as well.

Recipe does not work well with French cut green beans.

Directions

Set a large bowl of water with ice cubes, next to the sink, making sure to leave room in the bowl to add green beans later.

Place an empty colander in the bottom of the sink.

Using a large sauce pan, bring about one quart of water to a rolling boil on medium high heat.

Add 1 TSP salt to the boiling water.

Carefully place green beans in the boiling water for 2 minutes.

Remove the hot pan of boiling green beans from the stove and quickly pour the beans into a colander in the sink to drain, and then immediately pour the green beans into the ice water mix, as shown in picture **A**. Use a spoon to plunge the beans down into the ice water so that they are covered with the ice cubes floating on top.

Allow the green beans to rest in the ice water mix for at least 10 minutes.

In a large sauce pan, melt butter over medium heat, until it just barely starts to bubble. Add chopped shallots, garlic, and pepper and cook for one minute. Picture **B** shows the sauté butter mix with shallots and garlic.

Scoop the ice cubes out of the ice water mix and discard. Pour the green beans and water back into the colander to drain.

Add beans to the sauté butter mix, and continue cooking for two to three minutes, until the cold beans are heated through.

Serve immediately while hot.

Completed dish should appear as shown in small serving bowl in picture **C**.

A

B

C

"I wish I woulda" are very sad and regretful words. Go for it.

Corn Fiesta

Theodosia Surprise

Ingredients

Small 8-3/4 ounce can of corn

1-1/2 TBSP chopped onion

1 TBSP sweet pepper

1/2 TBSP white sugar

Pinch of salt

Pinch of black ground pepper (opt.)

Serves 2

A Bone from Pennie

Okay so now KNUCKLEHEAD I'm trying to figure out if you are crazy, stupid, or just plain can't read. The recipes don't get any easier than this one.

I chose to write this recipe for the small can of corn that serves 2 people. If you want to use the large can of corn, typically 15 ounces, then simply double the quantities of the other ingredients. All else remains the same, including cooking time.

The key to the recipe is the addition of the sugar.

If desired, add a tablespoon of butter about half way through the cooking time.

Any seasoning is suitable for this recipe. I have used the common salt and ground pepper, but I actually prefer to use an all purpose vegetable seasoning for this dish, along with a pinch of salt. Season to your taste.

Directions

The simple list of all the ingredients is shown in picture **A**.

Open the can of corn and pour the entire can, corn with liquid, into a small sauce pan.

Add all other ingredients. Picture **B** shows the dish with all of the ingredients in the pan, prior to turning on the heat. Set the heat to medium high.

Cook uncovered on medium high for 8 minutes, stirring frequently while the corn is heating. Do not allow the corn to scorch or burn, as most of the liquid will cook out of the dish.

When the corn has completed cooking, remove from the stove. Use a slotted spoon to remove the corn to a serving bowl.

The completed dish is shown in picture **C**. Serve while hot.

Go to the front of the line, and meet challenges and adversity head on with courage and integrity. No one respects, or wants to follow a man that cannot, or does not, do this.

Roasted Potatoes

Whetstone Accent

Ingredients

2 pounds of small fingerling potatoes

1/4 cup olive oil

1 TBSP Worcestershire sauce

Seasoning to taste

1 TSP paprika

2 TBSP minced garlic with juice

2 TBSP minced fresh rosemary

Serves 6 to 8

Note: For presentation purposes I have used half small butter potatoes, and half small red potatoes, so that you can see how each would appear in a completed dish.

A Bone from Pennie

This is a great and simple recipe KNUCKLEHEAD, so unless you want to become live bait for the neighbors meat grinder, pay attention and get this one correct.

If you are short on time, cut all the potatoes in half, and perform all other tasks the same, but cook for only 25 or 30 minutes.

The type of potato, as well as their size, will determine the actual cooking time. The forty minutes I have suggested, is an average time. Small or tender potatoes may take only 30 to 35 minutes, and larger or more firm potatoes may take 45 minutes or so. Check the potatoes for tenderness, while you are stirring them during the baking process.

At this temperature, it is safe to spray your baking dish with PAM, or line the baking dish with aluminum foil. Either will facilitate the clean up of the baking dish later.

Directions

Preheat oven to 375 degrees.

In a small mixing bowl, place the rosemary, seasoning to taste, and paprika. Stir to mix.

In a separate small mixing bowl, pour in the Worcestershire sauce, oil, and minced garlic.

The two bowls of prepared mixes are shown in picture **A**.

Wash and rinse potatoes. Do not slice or cut.

Place some olive oil in the palm of your hand, and hand rub each potato to coat the surface of the potatoes with a light coat of olive oil.

Place all potatoes in the bottom of a large baking dish.

Evenly drizzle the liquid oil, garlic, and Worcestershire sauce over all of the potatoes.

Immediately follow up with an even distribution of the dry ingredients mix of paprika, rosemary, and seasoning to taste, over the potatoes.

Your prepared dish at this time should look like the one shown in picture **B**.

Place the dish, uncovered, in the center of the preheated oven, set the timer for 40 minutes, and bake.

Potatoes should appear lightly browned, and be tender to a fork.

If your potatoes are stacked or layered, be sure and stir them a couple of times while they are baking.

Picture **C** shows the dish, after it has just been removed from the oven.

Serve while hot, as a side to any meat dish.

A

B

C

Nice words are not always truthful, and truthful words are not always nice.

60

Baked Beans

Little Creek Bam!

Ingredients

1 large can of pork and beans

2/3 cup ketchup

1/4 cup mustard

1/2 cup finely sliced fresh ham

1/4 cup diced onions

4 TBSP brown sugar

Serves 4 to 6

A Bone from Pennie

I couldn't find a "sarcasm" font KNUCKLEHEAD, but accept my compliments anyway, on what a magnificent chef and human being you have become.

I try to use the simplest of ingredients, so that you can prepare these dishes quickly and easily at home. Even though this dish may not look so appealing as you prepare it, (reference picture **B**) you will be pleasantly surprised and delighted with the final dish.

If you use the raw bacon option discussed, cut the bacon into bite size lengths of about 1-inch or so, before laying on top of the beans to bake.

Cooling the baked beans down for a few minutes before serving, allows the sauce to thicken just a little, and makes a better dish.

Large pieces of onion may not completely cook. Use small diced pieces.

Directions

Pre-heat oven to 400 degrees.

The few ingredients are all shown in picture **A**.

Using an oven safe dish, spray lightly with PAM non-stick spray, and pour in the pork and beans.

Add ham, onions, and brown sugar. Add the ketchup and mustard to the top surface, at which time your dish should look like the one shown in picture **B**. Very lightly stir the beans and sauce so as to mix well, but not break up the beans.

There are a couple of options available at this point, prior to baking. I like to some times add a few quarter size slices of ham on top of the beans. A more traditional option is to place strips of raw bacon on top. Either is fine, but be sure and add these pieces before baking the dish.

Cover tightly with aluminum foil or well fitted lid, and bake for 35 minutes, being sure to set the timer.

Carefully remove the dish from the oven with mitts or pot holders, and place on stove top to cool for a few minutes before serving. The dish should appear similar to my dish in picture **C**.

Serve while warm.

A

B

C

Never underestimate the power of determination and hard work, as it will often overcome others' talent and training.

Acorn Squash

Roy and Jessie's

Ingredients

1 large acorn squash

1/4 cup butter

1/4 cup brown sugar

3 TBSP Karo syrup (or honey)

1/2 TSP ground cinnamon

1/2 TSP vanilla

1/4 TSP salt

1/4 TSP ground nutmeg

Serves 4

A Bone from Pennie

Don't worry KNUCKLeHead, if you catch yourself on fire cooking the squash glaze, I promise to go in and clear your computer history before your friends and relatives get a hold of everything. Nobody needs to know, do they?

Once again I use a small pan covered with aluminum foil, in lieu of a standard baking dish, only because the clean up is easier. You can just as easily prepare the same dish without using foil if you desire.

If you undercook the glaze, it will still be fine to serve, but will have just a slight granular texture. Overcooking however will have somewhat of a scorched taste. If you scorch the glaze, throw it away, and start from scratch again.

This squash dish is so sweet, you may want to consider covering the finished squash quarters with a TBSP of chopped walnuts on each piece, and serve it as a dessert. It is superb!

Directions

Pre-heat oven to 350 degrees.

Accumulate ingredients shown in picture **A**.

Place the acorn squash on a cutting board, and carefully cut the squash in half. Use a spoon and clean out the seeds and fibrous material in the cavity of the squash, until your squash looks like the two halves shown in the picture.

Use olive oil to lightly coat the inside meat (yellow) part of each squash, and place the squash, cut side down, in a lined pan or baking dish, for baking. Place the dish in the oven uncovered and bake for 45 minutes, being sure to set the timer.

While the squash is baking, prepare the glaze as follows; place all other ingredients in a small sauce pan, and slowly bring up to temperature of medium heat setting. Boil slowly uncovered for about 5 minutes, stirring occasionally, until sugar is dissolved and non-granular in texture. Your liquid mix as it boils will look like the sauce being prepared in picture **B**.

Remove the squash from the oven, once baking time is complete, and allow to cool slightly, until you can handle the squash safely without burning yourself. Cut the halves in half, so that you now have 4 quarters of squash.

Using a knife, score the meat of the squash 3 or 4 times on each quarter, to allow the glaze to penetrate down into the meat of the squash.

Pour the glaze over the squash quarters, as shown in picture **C**.

Place the entire pan of glazed squash quarters back in the oven and bake for 5 additional minutes.

Remove squash and serve while hot. This dish is better than candy!

A

B

C

Remember that your family loves you. They may get mad at you, but they will still love you; no matter what.

Sweet Peas

Novella's Nuance

Ingredients

2 cups frozen green peas

1 TBSP butter

1/2 TBSP white sugar

1/4 cup of halved pearl onions

1/2 TSP salt

Pepper and seasoning to taste

Serves 2 to 3

A Bone from Pennie

I can only assume KNUCKLEHEAD, that you are planning on someone giving you a brain transplant for Christmas. Just in case that doesn't come through, lets learn to cook this simple little recipe so you won't starve in the mean time.

Canned sweet peas work fine with this dish, but are not as firm. The flavor of them however is fine.

If you scorch the peas, you will get an odor that will make your pet buzzard puke, and probably ruin your sauce pan. Do not let the peas get low on water, while you are heating the dish in the first step. Check every couple of minutes and add water as necessary.

The pearl onions are sweeter than normal onions, and add a little pizzazz to the appearance of the dish. However, substituting finely chopped onions or shallots (use only 1/4 cup) is an acceptable alternative substitute.

Directions

Accumulate ingredients as shown in picture **A**.

Using a large sauce pan, bring one cup of water to a rolling boil on stove top using a medium high setting.

Add frozen green peas and let water return to boiling, and then boil for 2 minutes.

Add all remaining ingredients, and boil for an additional 2 minutes.

Reduce heat to low, cover with lid, and allow dish to simmer for 5 minutes, as shown in picture **B** just prior to placing the lid on the sauce pan.

Use a slotted spoon to scoop the peas out and into a serving dish.

Picture **C** shows one serving of sweet peas in a small serving bowl.

This is a very quick, but very flavorful dish that can be prepared quickly on short notice.

If desired you can substitute some frozen corn or frozen carrots for some of the peas and make a mixed vegetable dish or a succotash. All other cooking directions remain the same.

Garnish with a very light drizzle of honey if desired, and serve while hot.

A

B

C

Know that you cannot always fight just the battles that you know you can win. Sometimes you have to fight the battles that are simply worth fighting.

Asparagusso

Clarence's Classic

Ingredients

1 bundle fresh asparagus (25/30 ct.)

Seasoning

Olive oil

Fresh shredded parmesan cheese

Serves 3 to 4

A Bone from Pennie

Yes KNUCKLEHEAD, people actually do eat asparagus, and some of us even love it when it is properly prepared. So pay attention, as poorly prepared asparagus, with parmesan cheese, can gag a maggot and make a skunk back up.

When selecting your fresh asparagus at the market, choose thinner stalks over thicker ones, and pay close attention to the heads that they are firm and not limp or soggy looking.

Olive oil is best for this dish, in my opinion, but a good quality vegetable oil is okay in a pinch.

Squirt a dash of fresh lemon juice on the top of the cheese for a little extra zip in the dish. Grating the lemon peel to a fine zest, can be added in moderation, if desired as well.

Use fresh shredded parmesan cheese, or buy a wedge of fresh parmesan, and grate it onto the asparagus.

Directions

Pre-heat oven to 350 degrees.

Gently rinse and clean the asparagus.

Place the asparagus on a clean cutting board and lop off the bottom one to two inches to remove the thicker areas of the stalk, and any brown areas on the bottom of the stems, as shown in picture **A**.

Place the asparagus in an oven safe container, and spread the stalks evenly across the bottom of the dish. Try not to layer if possible, but do not stack more than two high in any event.

Picture **B** shows the dish ready to go in the oven, after having drizzled olive oil over the top of it and seasoned it to taste. Be generous enough with the olive oil, going back and forth, that some of it lays on the bottom of the dish. Regular salt, and ground peppercorns are ideal, but most seasonings will work fine with this asparagus.

Do not cover, and place in the preheated oven for 15 minutes. Set the timer.

Remove the dish from the oven, remembering to use pot holders or oven mitts, and immediately sprinkle the fresh shredded or grated parmesan cheese onto the top of the asparagus.

Serve the dish as is, by placing it on a hot serving mat on the table, or if you choose, place the asparagus directly onto the entrée plate.

Picture **C** shows the completed dish, ready to serve and enjoy.

A

B

C

Make sure your children have a good education and love in their heart, and they will be fine, even when you are not around.

Red Beans & Rice

Daniel's Delicacy

Ingredients

1 pound dried red kidney beans

2 "*smoked*" pork chops

1-1/2 TBSP ham base stock

1 TSP salt

1/2 TSP pepper

4 bay leaves

1 TSP Tabasco hot sauce

2 TBSP olive oil

1/2 cup diced red onion or shallots

2 TBSP minced garlic with juice

1 pound sliced smoked sausage

3 cups cooked white rice

Serves 6 to 8

*** Author's favorite recipe

A Bone from Pennie

Easy with the hot sauce KNUCKLEHEAD. Too much can poison a whale and make a grown man cry, and parts of your body will hate you tomorrow.

Check the beans thoroughly as you rinse them. Discard any off color beans or any contaminants such as small rocks, which are common.

If you don't have time, or want to be lazy, then you can bypass the overnight soaking. Prepare the beans as per the recipe, and simply cook an additional 1 to 2 hours or so, until the beans reach the desired level of tenderness. If you use this option, do not add the sausage until halfway through the cooking time.

You can use any type of sausage. Cajun andouille sausage is traditional, but is very spicy. Italian sausage, any smoked sausage, or smoked ham hocks is acceptable.

These beans will refrigerate and keep for 3 or 4 days easily. Heat in microwave and serve over fresh rice.

Directions

Place 2 cups of dried red beans in a colander, in the sink, and rinse well.

Place beans in mixing bowl with 6 cups of water, add 1 TSP of salt and stir slightly, cover, and let stand overnight. You do not need to refrigerate. Two cups of dry beans when first placed in water are shown in picture **A** on the left. On the right is the same bowl of beans after soaking overnight, which now measures almost 4 full cups.

Pour the soaked beans into a colander and drain, but do not rinse. Place beans in large stock pot, and add exactly 8 cups of water.

Prepare sausage, by cutting links on a diagonal angle, into oval segments About 1/4-inch thick as seen in picture **B**. Cut the smoked pork chops into bite size pieces.

In a large sauce pan, brown the sausage on medium high for 2 minutes on each side. Turn the heat down to medium, add onions, garlic, and bay leaves, and simmer for 5 minutes, stirring occasionally.

Add all of the sauce pan ingredients and juices, into the stock pot with the beans and water. Turn the heat to medium high, and bring the liquid to a rolling boil. This may take about 10 minutes. Add all remaining ingredients, and allow the mixture to boil for 10 minutes.

Reduce the heat to low, cover with lid, and simmer for 3 hours. Check beans to see if they are soft. If not simmer an additional 30 minutes. Check beans periodically for loss of water. If mix is becoming too dry add a little chicken broth to bring up the level of liquid. Picture **C** is a one bowl serving.

Serve one large ladle full of beans and sausage, over 1/2 cup of rice as a side dish. If main course then larger servings are suggested. Garnish with parsley.

A

B

C

Life sometimes gives you a second chance. Take advantage and don't squander the new opportunity.

KNUCKLEHEAD NOTES:

Desserts For a Knucklehead

Bachelor, New Graduate, Beginner, and other Knuckleheads

Desserts are known to have salvaged many an average or poor meal. These recipes may help you salvage one of your meals, or may just be a wonderful indulgence of that sweet tooth that exists in all of us.

For ordinary day to day desserts such as cherry pie, chocolate cake, oatmeal cookies, etc., I suggest you go to the bakery section of your local grocery store. They have tried and proven recipes, that cost less money than you would probably spend to cook the same dishes. They are also convenient, and the only mess you have to clean up are the crumbs on the front of your shirt. For this reason, I have written and included the recipes for unusual desserts that you cannot find in a store. Don't miss my mom's famous chopped apple cake.

Chopped Apple Cake

My Mama's Best

Ingredients

1 cup flour

1 TSP baking soda

1 TSP cinnamon

1 TSP ground cloves

1/4 TSP salt

*****

1/4 cup shortening

1/3 cup oil

1 cup sugar

1 whole raw egg

*****

2 cups chopped apples

1/2 cup raisins

1/2 cup black walnut pieces

A Bone from Pennie

I grew up with my mom making this cake, and I love it KNUCKLEHEAD. It is my favorite dessert, so a word to the wise; never mind you don't qualify.

If you have an apple coring device, then core the apples before you pare them.

When paring an apple or any fruit or vegetable, go slowly and try to leave as much of the meat of the fruit as possible, and as little as possible with the peelings, as you will discard the peels when finished.

The thickness of the dough mix in the baking dish will affect the baking time. Stick a toothpick in the cake after 30 minutes of baking time, and withdraw it to inspect. If the toothpick has a lot of moisture or dough mix on it, then bake the cake for an additional 5 minutes or so. Do not over-bake, and leave the top crust a crisp golden brown.

Do not try and ice a hot or warm cake. It just doesn't work.

Directions

There are a lot of ingredients in this mix, as shown in picture **A**, but the recipe is really quite simple to make. Place the first five ingredients in a large mixing bowl and sift together or stir very well for even distribution.

Add the next four ingredients and mix on low speed until blended. This mix will be substantially drier and thicker than you are used to. In fact my mom makes this dish without using the oil, but I have added oil as it facilitates the mixing process.

The recipe calls for 2 cups of chopped apples. Depending on the size of apples, and how well you can pare the peeling off the apples, it will take approximately 3 regular sized apples to get two cups of chopped apples to add to the mix. Pare the skin from the apples first, discarding the peelings, and then split the apples in half. Cut the core from the apple halves, and then turn the apple halves over so you have a flat side laying on your cutting board. Carefully slice and dice to the size of apple pieces you desire. Dicing them to about the size of a pencil eraser is ideal and helps add more juice to the mix. I like larger pieces of apples for the texture and more crunch, as shown in picture **B** to the right, where I have added the apples, raisins and black walnuts to the dough mix. Gently fold, not stir, the ingredients all together so as not to break up the apple pieces.

Place the cake dough in a shallow baking dish that will keep the mix no less than 1-inch thick, and no more than 2-inches thick. Place the dish in a preheated oven at 350 degrees and bake for 30 minutes. This particular cake can be served hot without icing and is fabulous that way. If desired, purchase a can of sour cream whipped icing, and after the cake is cooled, cover the entire top with a layer of icing about 1/4-inch thick (sprinkling chopped walnuts onto the icing is a great addition). Cut into squares and serve.

A

B

C

Respect others and respect yourself as well. Take responsibility for your actions, and be accountable.

Snow Ice Cream

Missouri Madness

Ingredients

1 pot full of clean white snow

2/3 cup of milk

2 TSP vanilla extract

1/2 cup of sugar

4 raw eggs

Serves 4

A Bone from Pennie

DO NOT use yellow snow KNUCKLEHEAD. I'm not going to try and explain, just trust me on this one.

Brain Freeze! This dish is unbelievably cold and if you try and eat it too quickly it will instantaneously give you a head ache in your temples, that my kids endearingly referred to as brain freeze. I am sure you know what I am talking about, so be warned.

Snow has very different consistencies depending on the area of the country. Snow may come as large flakes or small flakes and may be dry or somewhat wet. For these reasons it may be necessary to adjust some of the quantities above. If it is too thick then add a little more milk and stir in. If it is too thin, then go get some more snow and add in the ice cream and mix it in well.

If you are squeamish about the raw eggs (don't be; you won't even know what they are when you eat this) then substitute egg beaters equivalent.

Directions

In a large mixing bowl, crack 4 raw eggs, and add milk and vanilla, as shown in picture **A**. Mix well with mixer on low to medium speed for about 1 minute.

Add sugar and mix again on low speed for about 1 minute.

At this point you should have a brown/yellow liquid that is a little more than one cup, similar to the standard measuring cup shown in picture **B**.

Go outside and obtain a full pot of snow, similar in size and quantity to the one shown in picture **B**.

You can mix the ice cream directly in the pot containing the snow, or transfer everything to a large mixing bowl if desired.

Obviously snow melts quickly at room temperature, so immediately upon bringing the snow inside, pour the liquid in the snow, and using a wooden spoon or soft spatula, immediately stir all the contents together.

As with the preparation, the serving of this dish must be immediate. The snow ice cream will not hold in a freezer without dramatically and permanently changing the consistency of the dish. You can hold it in a refrigerator for a very few minutes, but that is all.

Serve in a dish and enjoy homemade snow ice cream, just like our ancestors used to enjoy. One serving is shown in picture **C**.

WARNING: Since this dish contains raw eggs, it may not be kept and re-served later. Discard any unused ice cream. If you try and freeze the remainder it will melt and then freeze into a large rock hard ice cream cube. Don't bother.

A

B

C

Plan and save for your retirement now. Later is too late.

Fruit & Ice Cream

Kind Kim's

Ingredients

2 servings vanilla ice cream

1 cup fresh blackberries

1 TBSP butter

1 TBSP powdered sugar

2 TBSP honey

1 TBSP corn starch

1 TSP ground cinnamon

1 TSP ground nutmeg

1 TSP almond extract

Dash of flavored brandy (optional)

Serves 2

A Bone from Pennie

I know **Knucklehead**, that you don't think you need a recipe for this. Remember though, Custer didn't think he needed more troops. He was wrong and so are you (Big Surprise). Follow the recipe, and this will become one of your favorites.

You may use this same recipe for any small fruit such as strawberries, blueberries, raspberries, etc. The proportions of all the ingredients remain the same.

I try to keep the pan tilted to keep the sauce in a thicker puddle in the crease of the sauce pan, which assists in preventing over heating. When you see the bubbles in any of the heating phases, temporarily remove the pan to the side, allowing the sauce to cool for a few seconds, before resuming.

Don't try and measure the honey exactly to 2 TBSP. It is difficult to get it in and out of measuring spoons. Approximating the quantity is fine for this recipe, and add direct from the jar or squeeze bottle.

Directions

You need to have all of your ingredients accumulated (reference picture **A**) before starting this dish, and have them available near the stove cook top, as this recipe takes place quickly.

In a small sauce pan, melt the butter on low to medium heat. This sauce does not need to get very hot, just enough to melt the butter, but not scorch or burn.

Add the honey and allow to heat for one minute, stirring gently.

Add in 6 to 8 individual blackberries, and using a small table fork, smash them and break them up into the liquid, while keeping the sauce on a low heat. Cook for one minute.

Add the corn starch and stir slowly until the sauce begins to thicken.

Add all other ingredients in any order, stirring occasionally, and heat for another one minute.

When you see the sauce begin to bubble, immediately remove the sauce from the heat, as it is ready to serve. The sauce should be a burgundy color as shown in picture **B**. Do not over heat or overcook the sauce as it will begin to thin out.

Using two small serving bowls, place scoops of vanilla ice cream in the bowl. Split what remains of the one cup of blackberries between the two dishes, spreading the blackberries over the top of the ice cream. Do not stir or mix.

Pour the warm sauce over the two dishes of blackberries and ice cream, splitting evenly between the two dishes, and serve immediately.

Reference picture **C** for a suggested plating of the blackberries and ice cream.

A

B

C

Do not lie, cheat, or steal. It always comes back to bite you in some manner; if only your conscience.

Walnut Pie

Johnnie's Jewell

Ingredients

3 eggs

2/3 cup sugar

1/4 cup brown sugar

1/4 TSP salt

1 TSP vanilla extract

1 cup plain corn syrup

1/3 cup melted real butter

1 cup chopped English walnuts

1 9-inch pastry pie shell in baking tin

Serves 8

A Bone from Pennie

I know this is a more involved recipe, but really KNUCKLeHead, I have seen more potential for food preparation in a dyslexic chipmunk. Settle down and follow the directions, and you will have one of the most wonderful desserts ever to enter that pie hole you are licking right now.

This recipe can be used with walnuts or pecans. Be sure and buy raw unsalted nuts. They are usually in a plastic bag in the baking aisle of the market near the cake mixes and icing.

This is a great recipe to use with black walnuts, but if you have not cooked with them before, be aware that they have a very strong flavor, as opposed to the mild flavor of pecans or English walnuts.

You may use either a standard pie pastry pie crust, or the crunchy graham cracker variety. They are interchangeable and are simply a matter of personal preference.

Directions

Pre- heat oven to 350 degrees

Accumulate and prepare all the ingredients as shown in picture **A**, inclusive of melting the butter.

In a large mixing bowl crack and place the three raw eggs, and beat well at medium speed with mixer for 1 minute.

Add both sugars, salt, syrup, vanilla, and butter, and mix on medium speed again for 1 minute.

Add walnuts, and use spatula or wooden spoon to gently fold the walnuts into the mix, and reach an even and uniform mix of batter and walnuts.

Place the pastry pie shell, which comes in a baking tin, onto a cookie tray, and fill the pie shell with the prepared batter immediately. The batter should be about a 1/2 inch down from the top lip of the pie shell crust as shown in picture **B**.

As soon as oven is heated and ready, place the pie in the middle of the oven and bake for 50 minutes.

Set your timer and check the pie at 50 minutes by inserting a butter knife into the middle of the pie. It should come out clean. If moisture or batter sticks to the knife then continue baking for 3 minutes and inspect the pie again. Repeat the procedure until the knife comes out clean and the top of the pie is a golden brown color as in picture **C**. You must set your timer during this inspection phase of the recipe, as the pie will burn rather quickly once it has completed baking.

Remove the pie and allow to cool for at least 30 minutes before serving. It is okay if the pie filling runs a little, but if mixed and baked properly, the pie pieces should hold their shape once cooled.

Serve plain or with vanilla ice cream.

A

B

C

Don't back up. You never know how close to the wood chipper you may be.

Cherry Sponge Cake

Cherie Cheryl

Ingredients

1 box of 1-step angel food cake mix

1 22 oz. can cherry pie filling

1 can cream cheese frosting

Small amount of flour and Crisco

1/2 cup English walnuts chopped

Serves 8-12

A Bone from Pennie

I can tell you were born at an early age KNUCKLEHEAD, so I have included the simplest dessert recipe I know just for you.

This cherry sponge cake can be made very quickly and requires so little work that it is a great dessert when you are rushed or working with more involved entrée's and side dishes that require more of your time.

Do not use PAM or non-stick spray. You must grease the pan with a light coat of shortening or butter, and then sprinkle the flour onto the surface to coat the entire pan.

Hold the pan upside down over a garbage can after flouring, and gently tap the bottom of the pan to remove excess flour.

Be sure to wait at least 15 minutes after the cake comes out to cool, before applying icing.

Cake will be spongy in texture.

Directions

Pre-heat oven to 350 degrees.

Prepare your cooking pan for this recipe, by taking about a 15" X 10" inch jelly roll type pan with at least one inch high sides, and coat the pan with shortening or real butter. Use your hands for this and be sure to coat the entire pan with a fine layer of grease, before sprinkling flour onto the greased surfaces, as shown in picture **A**. Remove and discard excess flour.

Pour the contents of the angel food cake mix into a large mixing bowl, and add the entire 22 ounce can of cherry pie filling. Using a mixer on low, mix the contents thoroughly for 2 minutes.

The mix should be stiff and able to form ridges on the surface when stirred.

Pour the mix onto the greased and floured baking pan, as shown in picture **B**, making sure that the mix flows to all sides and corners. Do not leave any voids around the edges.

Place the baking pan in the middle of the pre-heated oven, and bake for 25 minutes.

Remove from oven and let cool for 15 minutes or longer, before icing.

Cover the entire sponge cake with icing. One full can should be more than enough to cover the entire dish. Sprinkle the nuts onto the icing, as shown in picture **C**. One serving of cooked sponge cake is shown without icing for reference of finished cake appearance. Serve by itself, or with vanilla or cherry ice cream, or with a sherbet of your choice.

OPTION: Instead of icing, use 1 cup of maraschino cherries in the fruit sauce recipe from page 70, and pour generous quantity over individual servings, (not the entire cake) when ready to serve.

There are young warriors who charge head on without regard, and there are old warriors who have learned the art of patience.

Upside-Down Apples

Tway's Tidbits

Ingredients

1/4 cup chopped walnuts

1/4 cup chopped dried fruit

2 TBSP brown sugar

1/2 TSP cinnamon

1/4 TSP nutmeg

1/2 TSP vanilla

4 TBSP honey

2 apples, halved and cored

Serves 4

Note: Any type of dried fruit may be used in this dish. I have used "Craisins"; sweetened dried cranberries with cherry flavor, produced by Ocean Spray, which are shown in the pictures.

A Bone from Pennie

Here you are KNUCKLEHEAD, a man unable to put his socks on in the dark, and I am trying to teach you how to make a dessert upside down. My fault; I forgot you were a big KNUCKLEHEAD! Perhaps if you pay attention to the directions, we can muddle our way through this one and let you end up with a great dessert.

Any dried fruit such as apricots, peaches, cherries, or any dried fruit combination, can be used.

Maple syrup can be substituted for the honey if you choose. The maple adds an extra flavor that is interesting, and may even be preferred.

All ingredients are edible before cooking, so don't over cook the dish. The baking is required to soften the apple and form a bonding glaze with the other ingredients.

Select a hard and firm variety of apple. I used *red delicious* in my preparation of the dish.

Directions

Pre-heat oven to 350 degrees.

Halve and core two apples. Do not peel.

Spray a 9-inch baking dish or pie pan with PAM, and accumulate all ingredients.

In a small mixing bowl place the nuts, fruit, cinnamon, and nutmeg. Gently stir these dry ingredients together to achieve a uniform mix.

As evenly as possible drizzle the vanilla over the mix, and then pour the contents into the prepared baking dish, spreading evenly across the bottom , as shown in picture **A**, as are the two apples on the left side of the picture, halved and cored.

Drizzle honey evenly and liberally over the top of the mixture, then evenly spread brown sugar across the mix.

Place the apple halves onto the nut and fruit mixture, cut side down, gently pressing them into the dried fruit mix, as shown in picture **B**.

Cover tightly with aluminum foil, or well sealing lid.

Place in pre-heated oven and bake for 35 minutes. Set the timer on the oven.

Remove from oven with pot holders, and remove covering.

Use a wooden spoon, or soft flat edged turner, separate the four halves, trying not to disturb the dried fruit now glazed to the apple halves.

Use a flat turner to pick up the separate pieces and place on serving plates, cut side up on apples.

Serve with scoops of vanilla ice cream, as shown in picture **C**.

Only about half of the dried fruit and walnuts will stick to the apple. Retrieve the pieces left in the dish, and either top off the apple halves, or spread over the ice cream as a garnish.

A

B

C

If you wish to convince someone that you are serious, or not afraid, then look them squarely in the eye, and hold their stare.

Caramel Corn

Terry Time

Ingredients

8 cups popped popcorn lightly salted

2 cup unsalted peanuts

2 cup packed brown sugar

1 cup butter

1 cup light corn syrup

1 TSP vanilla

1 TSP baking soda

Serves 8

Note: This is a large quantity that requires a large pan. Cut all quantities in recipe above by half, for a smaller more manageable quantity.

A Bone from Pennie

Did you ever wonder KNUCKLeHead, why so many people don't agree with you? It's because if they did, then you would both be wrong. Stop trying to outthink me here, and follow the recipe.

Before you ask; Yes I know this is not a dessert, and yes it is similar to crackerjacks, only better. So shut up and play ball.

Do not put any burned or un-popped kernels of popcorn in this mix.

Peanuts are an option. If you don't like them or want them, you can eliminate them from the mix, and follow all other directions exactly the same.

If you burn or scorch part of the popcorn, remove it from the batch and immediately discard in the trash. The rest of the popcorn will be fine, and should not pick up the burned flavor.

Directions

Pre-heat oven to 250 degrees.

Place popcorn in a deep roasting pan or on a cookie tray with a high lip. Add peanuts evenly throughout the popcorn.

In a large sauce pan mix sugar, butter, and corn syrup. Continually stir over medium heat, until the mixture begins to boil. Once the mixture begins to boil (mixture rolls around like a lava lamp) stop stirring. Allow the mixture to boil **without stirring** for 5 minutes. Remove from heat, and immediately stir in vanilla, and baking soda. Be prepared when you add the baking soda it will cause a miniature eruption of sorts, for about 2 seconds, and then stop. The caramel sauce, in a rolling boil, is shown in picture **A**.

While the caramel sauce is still hot, pour over the popcorn mix, trying to get an even distribution to coat all of the popcorn pieces, as shown in picture **B**. It will be necessary to immediately stir the popcorn with a wooden spoon, to allow complete coating of the popcorn kernels on all sides.

Place the popcorn mix in the preheated oven, uncovered, and bake for 60 minutes. Set your timer. You will need to continually stir the mix about every 10 or 15 minutes to keep the top layer from scorching, and bring the dripping sauce from the bottom, back up on top of the mix.

Remove the completed tray of caramel popcorn from the oven using oven mitts, and allow to cool for 30 minutes. Once cooled, use your hands to break up the mix into small individual pieces.

Place the completed dish of caramel popcorn in a storage container, with a good sealing lid, and store in a dark or cool place in the kitchen or the pantry. Picture **C**. shows a small serving dish of the completed caramel popcorn.

A

B

C

Always try to forgive your enemies. It annoys them to no end.

Snickers Surprise

> Jammin Jewell

Ingredients

1 box yellow cake mix

2 eggs

1/3 cup vegetable oil

1 bag mini snicker bars

Serves 8 to 12

A Bone from Pennie

The mind is like a parachute KNUCKLE-HEAD; it doesn't do you much good unless it is opened. So open your mind here to something a little bit unusual and outside the box, shall we say.

Chocolate cake mix can be substituted for the yellow cake mix, and is just as tasty (my mom's preference).

The cookie dough needs to be at least 1/4-inch thick on all sides of the snicker piece, to keep the snicker bar from melting and coming out of the dough and onto the cookie tray.

Kids absolutely love these snacks, but be careful with them getting too many, as they are very rich and filling.

It is better to undercook these, rather than overcook them, as they are somewhat gooey anyway. Over cooking makes the dough too crunchy, and over heats the snicker pieces.

Directions

Pre-heat the oven to 350 degrees.

Accumulate all ingredients as shown in picture **A**.

In a large mixing bowl, place the cake mix, eggs, and oil, and mix well at low speed.

Remove the small snicker bars from the packaging, and cut them in half. Take a piece of snickers, and about a heaping spoon full of cookie dough, and wrap the snicker piece with the dough, forming a small ball. Make sure the snicker piece is completely covered, and no chocolate is showing. The cookie ball, once formed should be slightly larger than a golf ball or a ping pong ball as a comparison. This procedure and final product, before baking, is shown in picture **B**. The consistency of the dough should be similar to that shown in the picture.

Place the cookie balls onto a non-stick cookie tray, spayed lightly with Pam, and bake for 12 minutes, or until cookie dough is cooked.

The final Snicker Surprise cookies are shown at the top of picture **C**, and a batch ready to bake, on a cookie tray, in the front of the picture.

These snicker surprise cookies can be served warm, or they can be kept and stored in sealed container, for 3 to 4 days if desired.

Two cookies are a serving.

A

B

C

Until one has loved an animal, part of their soul remains unawakened.

75

KNUCKLEHEAD NOTES:

Drinks For a Knucklehead

Bachelor, New Graduate, Beginner, and other Knuckleheads

You will quickly notice that I have utilized more pages for drinks than for any other section in this cookbook. Well we all have our weaknesses, don't we **Knucklehead**?

Most of the drinks on the first several pages of this section, are old time classics and favorites of the older generations. Not surprisingly, most bartenders today haven't heard of many of these drinks, and accordingly don't know how to prepare them either. However, they do usually keep a little bartenders cheat-sheet close by for reference, so don't be afraid to order these when you go out for drinks. If you are staying home, and just want to spice up your cocktail hour, or impress your friends, or whatever, then all the recipes you could possibly need are contained herein, and you won't have to flip a coin to see who's going to be the designated driver.

Classic Drinks I

Wake Up!

Ingredients

Vodka Drinks

Vodka is a very refined and filtered liquor usually distilled at 180 to 190 proof, before being bottled at 80 to 100 proof. Originally thought to have been developed in Russia and made from potatoes, vodka is now produced world wide and distilled from various grains inclusive of corn and wheat.

The filtering process and different grains gives vodkas there subtle differences in flavor. The newly developed "flavored" vodkas are sweetened with various fruit juices.

A Bone from Pennie

Yes it is true, **Knucklehead**, that some people actually prefer something to drink other than a beer, surprising and offensive as that may seem to you.

Bloody Mary's are traditionally served for brunch or morning drinks. Myth erroneously has hailed them as a cure for hangovers, but in my opinion are mainly just an excuse to drink in the morning, and are more than capable of causing, and not curing, a hangover.

Harvey Wallbanger. No explanation necessary, as the name says it all. Two of these are plenty, even for the heartiest of drinkers.

A *Salty Dog* is a simple and quickly made drink that is particularly refreshing in hot weather. The large amount of citrus juice in these can upset the stomach if over indulgence is the direction of the day. Not to be confused for "the hair of the dog", this drink is also commonly served as an early or mid morning eye opener.

Directions

Bloody Mary:

1.5 oz. Vodka

3 oz. tomato juice

1/2 tsp. Worcestershire Sauce

3 drops Tabasco Sauce

Add all in large cocktail glass, pepper and salt to taste, add celery stalk, squirt of lemon, and stir.

Harvey Wallbanger:

1 oz. Vodka

4 oz. Orange Juice

1 oz. Galliano

Mix vodka and orange juice well and pour over ice in tall glass. Add Galliano slowly to top of drink and allow to rest 1 minute before serving.

Salty Dog:

1.5 oz. Vodka

4 to 6 oz. Grapefruit Juice (red or yellow)

Rub the rim of cocktail glass with lemon peel or grapefruit section, and press rim down into loose salt. Pour ingredients over ice, and add 2 or 3 small shakes of salt to the drink itself if desired. Garnish with grapefruit segment and a fresh mint leaf, if available.

Beware the demons of alcohol and drugs, for when you dance with the devil, the devil never changes, but you do.

78

Classic Drinks II

Carl's Nips

Ingredients

Vodka Drinks

Vodka is rarely aged, and is considered suitable for consumption upon bottling at the selected Proof. This liquor is odorless and almost tasteless except to the very refined and trained palates of professionals.

Russians will tell you that vodka is meant to be drank straight and served cold in a small shot glass, and compliments most foods. Americans have found it to be best served in fruity drinks, where the flavor of the juices dominate the taste.

A Bone from Pennie

I have my spam filter wound all the way up to *Ultimate Knucklehead*, and still the e-mails like yours get through. Unbelievable.

A *Screwdriver* is one of the most popular drinks in America. Made with only two components, it is both quick and refreshing. I highly recommend a pure real orange juice. For a small twist, try stirring in one TSP of white powdered sugar, to sweeten the orange juice.

The *Vodka Collins* is the same as the popular Tom Collins, but substitutes vodka for the gin. Both famous and popular in the 50's and 60's it is not commonly ordered in bars today.

Black Russians have long been a popular drink for upscale gatherings, perhaps owing much to the intriguing and enchanting name. Watch your intake of these, as they can be unsettling to a sensitive stomach.

Directions

Screwdriver:

2 oz. vodka

4 to 6 oz. fresh orange juice

Pour both over ice in medium size cocktail glass, and stir well. Garnish with orange slice and serve immediately.

Vodka Collins:

2 oz. vodka

4 to 6 oz. tonic or carbonated water

A squirt (1 tbsp.) of lemon juice

1 tsp. powdered sugar or equivalent

Mix and pour over ice in tall glass and stir slightly. Garnish with maraschino cherry and a orange slice.

Black Russian:

1.5 oz. vodka

1 to 1.5 oz. kahlua (or coffee flavored liqueur)

Mix lightly and serve over ice in small cocktail glass. If desired, add 1.5 oz. of cream and you have a White Russian.

A

B

C

May your glass be ever full. May the roof over your head be always strong. And may you be in heaven half an hour before the devil knows you're dead.

Classic Drinks III

Good Night Irene

Ingredients

Rum Drinks

Yo-ho-ho and a bottle of rum. Aye mates, rum is thought to have been developed in the Caribbean west Indies. Made from sugar cane syrup and molasses, our pirate and naval ancestors soon adopted this drink for its flavor and easy transport to Europe and the colonies in America.

Rum is typically aged in wood barrels, and bottled at 80 to 100 proof. Caramel is often added for coloring or sweetness, and it is common for various rums to be blended together for flavor.

A Bone from Pennie

Knucklehead, would you describe yourself as an underachiever or merely a simpleton? Well no matter, as these recipes, though sophisticated, are quite simple.

A *Sidecar* is also an older drink, and was a common order for the Hollywood socialites in mid 20th century. The drink is a small quantity but powerful, and meant to be sipped much like a martini.

I enjoy ordering a *Corkscrew* just to say it and watch the bartenders reaction. Somewhat uncommon, this was the drink of choice of someone who wanted to be different and liked a very strong drink.

The *Cuba Libre'*, along with the Mojito, is the drink of choice for many Hispanics and is especially popular in the Miami and South Beach area. Simple, quick, and inexpensive it is a very refreshing cola drink. Crushed ice works best in this drink, but any kind of ice will work.

Directions

Sidecar:

3/4 oz. triple sec

1.5 oz. brandy

Squirt of lemon juice (or juice 2 lemon wedges)

Pour all three parts into a shaker, add ice and shake well. Strain contents into a martini or cocktail glass and garnish with lemon slice.

A

Corkscrew:

1.5 oz. rum

0.5 oz. dry vermouth

0.5 oz. Peach Brandy

Pour all three parts into a shaker, add ice and shake well. Strain contents into a martini or cocktail glass and garnish with a lime slice.

B

Cuba Libre':

2 oz. rum

4 oz. cola

Lime juice

Cut one lime in half. Squeeze half lime hard and drop the rind in a large cocktail glass with the juice. Pour rum onto the rind and add ice and cola and stir lightly.

C

May all those present love you, and if they don't love you may God turn their hearts, and if he can't turn their hearts, may he turn their ankles so we know them by their limp.

80

Classic Drinks IV

Aloha

Ingredients

Rum Drinks

Dark rums are generally found to be sweet and to have a heavy and abundant bouquet or aroma. These characteristics come from a slower fermentation process, which allows for the sugar and or molasses to develop and enrich the rum.

These sweet dark rums became the leading export of the West Indies in the 18th and 19th centuries, and quickly became the favorite import of America and Great Britain.

A Bone from Pennie

Marry soon **Knucklehead**. You need someone to take care of you now, and to count the pills for you later.

The *Mai Tai* is one of the more involved drinks to make. Traditionally a sweet almond syrup is used, but simple syrup, common in bars, is often substituted. In Hawaii this drink will often be topped with 0.5 oz. of 151 proof rum and then served with an orchid on top. Mai Tai's are traditionally served with a straw.

A *Cajun Crippler* is a drink I learned to enjoy when I lived in Cajun country for about 10 years. It is quite similar to a wine cooler and is a nice summer thirst quencher.

Popular in southern beach resorts and the Caribbean the *Rum Runner* is well known. Try adding a touch of blackberry brandy or sloe gin for extra flavor. These drinks pack a powerful wallop, and with the liquor hard to taste or detect, can be very inebriating to the unwary.

Directions

Mai Tai:

2 oz. rum

1 oz. triple sec

1 tbsp. each of syrup, grenadine, and lime juice

Mix all ingredients in shaker with ice, and shake well. Using a cocktail glass or tall glass filled half way with crushed ice, strain shaker contents over ice. Garnish with cherry and pineapple on spear.

A

Cajun Crippler:

1.5 oz. rum

1 oz. orange juice

0.5 oz. lemon juice

4 oz. (approx.) ginger ale or seven-up

Mix first three ingredients in shaker with ice and shake well. Pour into tall glass over ice, add ginger ale, and stir. Garnish with lemon slice.

B

Rum Runner:

1 oz. rum

1.5 oz. each of orange and pineapple juice

0.5 oz. grenadine

0.5 oz. banana liqueur

Mix well and serve over ice in tall glass. Garnish with orange slice.

C

Drink is the curse of the land. It makes you fight with your neighbor. It makes you shoot at your landlord, and it makes you miss him.

Classic Drinks V

Pat O'Brien's

Ingredients

Rum Drinks

Light rums, true to their namesake, are lighter in color than the dark rums, and will not typically have as sweet or heavy of a bouquet.

These rums are a favorite for many of the exotic tropical mixed drinks found at beach resorts throughout the world today. It was not unusual for smugglers to package the light rums as turpentine or related naval products, and often the raw rum taste very closely resembled those products.

A Bone from Pennie

Well, well, well. Zippy the total KNuCKLeHead has decided to try and add a little class to his new drink repertoire.

The *Pina Colada* is usually preared as a frozen drink. They are great summertime beverages, but beware of brain freeze if you try and drink this too fast.

The *Hurricane* can also be made in a blender as a frozen drink, and then served. Long a staple of Bourbon Street in New Orleans, many a light drinker has gotten lost in the subtlety of hurricanes and errantly disregarded the large amount of liquor in this drink.

A *Hot Buttered Rum* is believed to have been originated in England, and became a popular "nightcap" for plantation owners of the Old South. These drinks are very flavorful, and great cold weather drinks, but one is enough, as they are very rich.

Directions

Pina Colada:

3 oz. rum

3 tbsp. coconut milk

3 tbsp. crushed pineapple

Place ingredients in a blender with 1 cup of ice and blend on high speed for 10 seconds or until foam begins to form. Pour in tall glass and serve with straw. Garnish with slice of pineapple and a cherry.

A

Hurricane:

1 oz. each of dark rum and light rum

1 TBSP grenadine

3 oz. passion fruit juice

2 oz. almond or simple syrup

Mix ingredients well and pour over crushed ice in tall glass or hurricane bowl glass. Garnish with full wheel of lime and serve with straw.

B

Hot Buttered Rum:

2 oz. rum

2 tbsp. sugar or powdered sugar

1 pad of real butter

Use small coffee mug or cocktail glass. Add ingredients and fill rest of glass with water. Place in microwave to heat but not boil (about 30 seconds or until butter melts). Add dash of cream, stir well, and serve.

C

If you cheat, may you cheat death. If you steal, may you steal a woman's heart. If you fight, may you fight for a brother. If you drink, may you drink with me.

Classic Drinks VI

Siesta Beach

Ingredients

Rum Daiquiri's

Daiquiris were once considered a "ladies" drink, consisting of rum and fruit juice, blended with ice. The drink grew in popularity with the emergence of blenders, and was soon found to tastefully embrace almost any fruit or juice.

The most popular daiquiris arguably are strawberry, banana, and pineapple, but passion fruit and virtually all berries and fruits are currently used to make them; most notably at specialized daiquiri bars.

A Bone from Pennie

You know KNUCKLEHEAD, you don't have a whole lot going for you over those ice cubes in the blender. Pay attention and don't blend your fingers by mistake.

A *Strawberry* Daiquiri is one of the most common and popular frozen drinks in America. It can be made with either frozen or fresh strawberries, noting that fresh strawberries require less blending time.

The *Banana Daiquiri* is not as popular as the strawberry daiquiri, but has an acquired taste for anyone that likes and enjoys bananas. Be sure and note the slow speed of the blender in the recipe and do not over blend.

A *Daiquiri* can be made with almost any fruit, berry, or melon. This is a fun drink to get creative with and try some new combinations, and develop your own favorite daiquiri recipe. A melon daiquiri is shown in "C", and the liqueur substitute used was peach flavored brandy.

Directions

Strawberry Daiquiri:

2 oz. rum

1/2 cup each of frozen strawberries, and ice

1 tbsp. sugar

1 oz. lime juice

Place ingredients in blender on high for 10 seconds, pour in champagne glass, serve with straw, and garnish with large strawberry and a cherry.

A

Banana Daiquiri:

2 oz. rum

1/2 cup each of banana and ice

1 tbsp. sugar

1 oz. banana liqueur

Place ingredients in blender on low for 10 seconds, pour in champagne glass, serve with straw, and garnish with slice of banana and a cherry.

B

Daiquiri of Choice:

2 oz. rum

1/2 cup each of desired fruit and ice

1 tbsp. sugar.

1 oz. of complimenting liqueur or simple syrup

Place ingredients in blender on low for 10 seconds, pour in champagne glass, serve with straw, and garnish with slice of fruit and a cherry.

C

I have known many a lady, and liked but not a few; but loved only one my dear, and this toast is for you.

Classic Drinks VII

Queenies Quicksand

Ingredients

Whiskey Drinks

Whiskey is derived from a fermented grain mash of barley, wheat, corn, or rye, etc. Once distilled, whiskey is normally aged in oak barrels from one to ten years or longer.

There are very specific laws governing the distilled proof of whiskey, but in general whiskey will have a range in alcohol content from 80 to 110 proof.

Most whiskies are clear when distilled, and gain their color and flavor from aging in the oak barrels.

A Bone from Pennie

You have met the enemy KNUCKLeHead and it be you.

Considered a drink of a gone by era, the *Rob Roy* is a specialty drink often ordered by the older generation. It is quick to mix and just as quick to disable the overindulgent drinker. A very close cousin to the martini, it is made today with a variety of whiskies but most commonly, and traditionally, scotch whiskey.

The *Manhattan* is one of the old time favorites from the early 20th century that continues to be a patron favorite in bars today. These are powerful drinks and should be sipped and consumed in small quantities. It is made with both blended whiskey and scotch whiskey.

You better find an old time bartender, if you want to find one that has even heard of a *Horse's Neck* cocktail, let alone knows how to make one. This is a fun drink, and unique both in appearance and taste.

Directions

Rob Roy:

1.5 oz. scotch whiskey

0.5 oz. each of dry vermouth and sweet vermouth

Dash of bitters

Pour ingredients in shaker with ice and shake vigorously. Strain into martini glass and garnish with lemon peel and a cherry.

A

Manhattan:

1.5 oz. favorite whiskey

1 oz. sweet vermouth

Pour ingredients in shaker with ice, and shake vigorously. Strain into martini glass and garnish with a cherry on a spear.

B

Horse's Neck:

3 oz. of favorite whiskey

4 to 6 oz. seven-up or ginger ale

1 tsp. powdered sugar

Peel an entire lemon in a spiral fashion with the peel segment about a quarter inch wide. Place the entire peel section in a tall glass with peel hung on tip lip of the glass, add a small squeeze of the lemon juice. Pour in ingredients with whiskey first, add ice, and garnish with cherry.

C

Here's to women's kisses, and to whiskey amber clear. Not as sweet as a woman's kiss, but damn sure more sincere.

84

Classic Drinks VIII

Beach Ball Buster

Ingredients

Tequila Drinks

Tequila, also known as "to-kill-ya", has long been the staple drink of Mexico and distilled most notably in the town of Tequila, Mexico. Derived from the distilled juice of blue-agave plants, tequila is a very strong clear or amber colored liquor, traditionally served straight up in shot glasses at room temperature.

Today various mixed drinks have evolved using tequila as the core liquor, and many people now consume shots of tequila from bottles kept in a freezer as well. It is still possible today to buy the legendary bottle of tequila with a caterpillar worm in the bottom of the bottle.

A Bone from Pennie

One tequila, two tequila, three tequila, floor. This is the new math for KNUCKLEHEADS who over indulge from this page.

The *Margarita* is unquestionably the favorite drink of Mexico and a staple of Mexican restaurants everywhere. I have given you the recipe to make margaritas from scratch with fresh ingredients, but there are a number of pretty good Ready-Made-Mix products that are faster and more easily transported or stored.

Mistakenly ordered as a hangover cure, much like the Bloody Mary, a *Tequila Sunrise* causes more hangovers than it cures. Drink this in a clear glass, and enjoy a fun drink as it develops.

A *Tequini Cocktail* is not one of the better known tequila drinks, but it is, none the less, one of the better ones. Often served at high-end Mexican restaurants or bars, this too is a powerful drink and meant to be drank slowly.

Directions

Margarita:

3 oz. tequila

1 oz. triple sec

3 oz. lime juice

Rub lime peel around rim of margarita glass and coat rim with salt. Place ingredients in shaker with ice and shake vigorously, then pour into salt-rimmed glass. Garnish with slice of lime.

A

Tequila Sunrise:

2 oz. tequila

4 oz. orange juice

3/4 oz. grenadine

Add tequila, orange juice, and ice to shaker, and pour foamy mix with ice cubes into a clear cocktail glass. Add grenadine slowly and wait one minute, allowing grenadine to settle. Stir cocktail when ready to drink. Shown unstirred.

B

Tequini Cocktail:

3 oz. Tequila

1 oz. dry vermouth

3 dashes of bitters

Place ingredients in shaker with ice and shake well. Strain into martini glass and garnish with twisted lemon peel and olive on a spear.

C

Here's to our wives and girlfriends...May they never meet.

Classic Drinks IX

Hangover hits

Ingredients

Gin Drinks

Gin, not unlike other liquor, is distilled from grain, but receives its flavor from berries, most notably juniper berries.

Gin is typically clear, but can have a mild amber color, and was almost certainly the liquor of choice in the mid 1900's. So much so that bars and such became popularly known as gin mills.

Gin usually has a lower proof of 80 to 90. Often drank straight, gin today is more commonly mixed.

A Bone from Pennie

Two ounces of gin means two ounces of gin you KNUCKLEHEAD. It does not mean one ounce for the little people and 3 ounces for "*moi*".

The *Tom Collins* was one of the most oft ordered drinks of the 60's and 70's. Somewhat old fashioned today, you can see how it serves as a basis for the other two gin drinks.

Having lived in Singapore for two years, the *Singapore Sling* became my favorite exotic drink. Sloe gin is a common substitute for the brandy in this recipe.

Who doesn't like the old movie Casablanca? Listen closely in the reruns and you will here the bar patrons in Rick's Bar ordering a *French 75*. Still a popular upscale drink today, the French 75 is served regularly on the west coast of the U.S., especially in the San Francisco area. Like a mimosa, this drink can be served with brunch, or as an early morning eye opener.

Directions

Tom Collins:

2 oz. gin

1 tsp. powdered sugar

3 tbsp. lemon juice

4 to 6 oz. tonic or carbonated water

Mix and pour over ice in tall glass, garnish with lemon slice and cherry, and serve with a straw.

A

Singapore Sling:

2 oz. gin & cherry flavored brandy

1 tsp. powdered sugar & 1 TBSP grenadine

3 tbsp. lemon juice

4 to 6 oz. tonic or carbonated water

Similar mix as Tom Collins above, but at end, slowly float 2 oz. cherry flavored brandy on top. Garnish with cherry and fruit slices; add a straw.

B

French 75:

2 oz. gin

1 tsp. powdered sugar

3 tbsp. lemon juice

4 to 6 oz. champagne

Same mix as Tom Collins as well, but champagne substituted for tonic. Garnish with orange or lemon, add two cherries and serve with straw.

C

May misfortune follow you the rest of your life, but never catch up.

Classic Drinks X

Thirst Quenchers

Ingredients

Specialty Drinks

One of the more common terms used with gin is the descriptive adjective "dry". Dry gin simply means that the gin has had little or no sweetness added, and is very popular for martinis.

Flavored gins have gained in popularity over the past few decades, and flavors such as peach, apricot, orange, and lemon are common. Oddly enough sloe gin, a deep red heavy bodied liquor, is not a gin at all, but rather a liqueur made from sloe plums.

A Bone from Pennie

No Knucklehead, these are not drinks they serve to "Special" people like yourself. My Irish friend once told me that the difference between an Irish wedding and an Irish funeral is that the funeral has one less drunk. The moral of the story being; moderation is the best policy with these drinks.

If you have never tried an *Irish Coffee*, then you are missing out on what is arguably the most popular hot drink served. Great for a night cap or at the end of a rich meal, this drink, properly prepared, can almost substitute for dessert.

There are literally hundreds of cooler recipes. I chose the *Rum Cooler*, mainly for its simplicity as well as thirst quenching characteristics.

I am including the *Charlie Chaplin*, having never had one until researching this book, and thought it unusual in both ingredients and taste. Yes it is named for the one and only Charlie Chaplin; reportedly his favorite.

Directions

Irish Coffee:

2 oz. Irish whiskey (or favorite whiskey)

1 cup hot black coffee

1 tbsp. sugar

Use a large coffee mug, or tall clear glass, wet the rim, and coat with sugar. Pour in whiskey first and fill to 3/4 full with hot strong coffee. Add whipped cream to top, and serve with straw.

[A]

Rum Cooler:

2 oz. rum

1 tbsp. powdered sugar

4-6 oz. seven-up or ginger ale.

2 squeezed slices of lemon or lime

Mix together well and pour over fruit slices, and ice in tall glass. Garnish with lime or lemon slice, or sprig of fresh mint, and serve with straw.

[B]

Charlie Chaplin:

2 oz. sloe gin

2 oz. apricot flavored brandy

2 oz. lemon juice

Place all ingredients in shaker with ice, and shake well. Shake well and pour drink and ice in small cocktail glass, and garnish with lemon slice and cherry.

[C]

May you die in bed at 95 years of age; shot by a jealous wife.

Jason's Punches

Mind Quenchers

Ingredients

Exotic Punches

Fruit punch and liquor mixes have been around as long as anyone can trace, with references to these concoctions as far back as medieval times. Almost all fruit juice and fruit juice combinations are compatible with some variety of rum, vodka, or gin.

Perhaps the most popular or well known punch is a "champagne punch", which is one of the recipes on this page, and very commonly found at bridal receptions, and other formal events.

A Bone from Pennie

Be careful with drinking too much from this page KNUCKLEHEAD. I know you know where you are right now, but too much of these and I can assure you that you will view the room from a different angle.

These are nice moderate punches to serve at more sophisticated events that you might be invited to, or be a part of, by mistake.

The *Champagne Punch* continues to be one of the most often served punches in America at festive gatherings. There are enumerable versions of this old stand by recipe.

Planter's Punch is still very popular today. I am giving you a single drink recipe in lieu of entire bowl, to allow you to enjoy this drink at home.

Boom Boom Punch is called by many names, but I have chosen this one in hopes you will be careful in how many cups you serve your crazy aunt.

Directions

Champagne Punch:

1 cup triple sec

2 cups brandy

2 cups of seven-up or ginger ale

2 bottles champagne

1 8-12 oz jar of maraschino cherries with juice

Mix all in punch bowl, pouring champagne in last, and add ice as desired. Decorate with floating circles of fruit such as lemon, lime, and orange.

A

Planter's Punch:

2 oz. each of light rum and dark rum

Juice 1 each lemon, lime, and orange

1 tbsp. each of pineapple juice and sugar

2 dashes of triple sec

Mix all ingredients and pour over ice in tall glass. Add fruit slice(s), and serve with straw.

B

Boom Boom Punch:

2 bottles of rum

1 bottle each of sweet vermouth and champagne

1 quart of orange juice (2 quarts for weaker mix)

Mix all ingredients in punch bowl, adding champagne last. Add ice as desired, and float sliced banana and orange wheels in punch.

C

A toast to your coffin. May it be made of 100 year oak, and may we plant the tree together, tomorrow.

Crystal's Creations

Seatbelts Please

Ingredients

Booze: (and lots of it)

Creative drinks have been around as long as stupid people have been around, and that's a long time.

Trying to find new and creative ways to serve or disguise your favorite liquor has been a pass time for many a year. Several new beverage makers promote their products by finding new mixes of their beverage with liquors, to help promote sales. This is especially popular today with the enormous new emerging market of *energy* drinks.

A Bone from Pennie

OMG. I was hoping you would not find this page KNUCKLEHEAD. Perhaps you should call the police station downtown and pre-register for a nights stay.

Yes a *Skippy* is a real drink that was developed, to my knowledge, by my friends in Bradenton, Florida. Surprisingly, you do not taste the beer, and this is a great summertime drink.

The *Screaming Monkey* is very aptly named, as it most closely approximates the actions of a friend of mine who drank three of these.

I added this drink, just because I liked the name. A friend of mine in Texas had actually tried this drink before, and warned me that the *Flying Grasshopper* is very very rich and very very strong. As he explained, if you drink too many of these, there will come a time when you think you are going to die, and a time shortly thereafter when you are afraid you won't.

Directions

Manatee Skippy

Frozen lemonade concentrate—1 can

Vodka—1 can full (empty lemonade can)

2 bottles of beer (any kind/not dark)

Empty a full can of frozen lemonade concentrate into a large pitcher. Fill can with vodka and pour on top of concentrate. Pour beer slowly, not to foam, and stir. Serve over ice with lemon slice.

Screaming Monkey

1 oz. vodka

1 oz. Raspberry Schnapps.

2 oz. pineapple Juice

1 oz. almond syrup or simple syrup

Place in shaker with ice and shake lightly. Serve neat or over crushed ice, and garnish with slice of pineapple and cherry.

Flying Grasshopper

1 oz. vodka

1 oz, crème de menthe

1 oz. white crème de cacao

Place all in shaker with ice and shake lightly. Strain into martini glass and garnish with sprig of fresh mint and a cherry.

Here's to me and here's to you. Here's to health and the wealth you're due. Here's to women who are never blue. Here's to love may it cling like glue. Cheers my friend.

DONN'S DIZZIES

Tina's Tini's

Ingredients

Martini's

The martini has always borne the legend of being a powerful drink, but in fact is no more powerful than any other drink of the same alcohol content.

Martinis were originally a half and half drink of gin and vermouth. A popular drink of the movie stars in the World War II era, drier martini recipes evolved using more gin than vermouth, olives added, and eventually vodka substituted for gin as well. The less vermouth, the drier the martini.

A Bone from Pennie

Please put down the beer while you are trying to make some decent drinks. Really KNUCKLEHEAD, I think an intoxicated yak in Nepal may have more class than you demonstrate.

The *Martini* is almost held in reverence by legend, and is probably the best known drink in America. Famous since the early 1900's there are many variations of this drink today, and vodka is now commonly substituted for gin as a matter of personal preference.

The *Gibson Martini* bears no difference from the original martini except for the garnish of the pearl onions. You have to wonder what brave soul came up with that idea, and I can only speculate that it was a very daring Mr. Gibson.

An *Apple-Tini*, or Apple Martini is one of many of the popular new martinis developed with the emergence of flavored vodka. This is a tart drink, but very refreshing.

Directions

Original Martini:

Gin and dry vermouth (in this order for following)

Traditional martini is 2 : 1 or 3 to 1 ratio

Dry martini is about a 5 : 1 ratio

Very dry martini is 8 : 1 ratio (splash of vermouth)

Place exact amount of ingredients desired in shaker with fresh ice. Shake well for 5 seconds and strain into martini glass. Garnish with olives.

Gibson Martini:

Use the recipe above for either the dry martini or extra dry martini.

Place exact amount of ingredients desired in shaker with fresh ice. Shake well for 5 seconds and strain into martini glass. Garnish with pearl onions on a spear and a twist of lemon rind if desired.

Apple-Tini:

2 oz. Green apple vodka

1 oz. sour apple schnapps

Follow directions for regular martini, but garnish with a slice of green apple either floated in drink or on rim of martini glass.

A

B

C

A man shall nay be drunk if he can find his arse with both hands, and his girlfriends with one.

Nautical Nemeses'

Crazy Art

Ingredients

Lots of Liquor

It was not sailors that developed loneliness and the comfort of drink at sea, but liquor has long been associated with the nautical life. Rum, ale, and grog were part of the daily rations in the old English and French naval forces, and more than one riot erupted on ships from improper or lack of proper refreshment.

Designated drivers are not just for automobiles, but very appropriate for boats as well. Bon Voyage and happy safe boating.

A Bone from Pennie

I don't want to hear any of that nonsense, KNUCKLEHEAD, claiming you didn't over drink, but that you must have been "over served". These drinks are very strong, and not meant for chugging contests.

My neighbor in New Orleans used to make *Fog Cutters* for us after a day of golf, and I grew to really enjoy the taste of them. A lot of citrus juice in these, so be moderate in your consumption on an empty or sensitive stomach.

Damn The Weather is an old recipe that was popular in the European nautical communities many years ago. Still a favorite of the hard line sunrise drinkers, it is both tasty and refreshing.

The *Admiral's Toddy* is a famous old "Skipper's" recipe and both gin and Irish whiskey are commonly substituted for the brandy, based on individual preference. Damn the torpedoes and full speed ahead.

Directions

Fog Cutter:

1.5 oz. rum

0.5 oz. each of brandy and gin

1 oz. each of orange juice and lemon juice

1 tbsp. simple syrup

Mix all in shaker with ice and strain over fresh ice in tall glass, top with splash of sweet sherry, and garnish with a cherry and slice of lemon.

Damn The Weather:

1.5 oz. gin

1 tbsp. each of sweet vermouth and orange juice

1 tsp. triple sec

Place all ingredients in a shaker with ice and shake vigorously for 10 seconds. Strain and pour into martini glass or cocktail glass and garnish with orange slice. Can be served over ice.

Admiral's Toddy:

2 oz. brandy

4 oz hot water (coffee temperature)

1 tbsp. sugar

Mix all in coffee mug and heat in microwave if necessary, but do not boil. Squeeze a slice of lemon and drop into drink. Lightly sprinkle some nutmeg on top, for an added touch.

A

B

C

We drink to each others health this night, knowing that good drink is only for those of us who can afford to lose the brain cells. Cheers my friend.

Shooters

Jail Time Jollies

Ingredients

You don't really want to know

The history of "Shooters" seems clouded, but we do know their popularity has increased dramatically since 1980 or so, and are now the poison of choice at most college campuses.

Shooters can range from straight booze such as tequila or vodka, to various exotic mixes of an unbelievable variety of liquids. There are quite literally hundreds of shooters, so I have chosen to list 3 of the more popular choices.

A Bone from Pennie

FYI **Knucklehead**, *shooters* are not so named because you throw them down your gullet in one shot, but because of what they make you want to do to yourself the next morning. Two of these is plenty, and three will head you in the direction of trouble. No I don't know what kind of trouble, but rest assured you will find out if you try and over do it here.

As I mentioned above, there are hundreds, if not thousands, of shooter recipes, and without question too many to try and list them all in this limited setting. Shooters are known as much for their hilarious and provocative names as for their surprisingly good flavor. I have chosen 3 of the most popular shooters, utilizing many of the same ingredients to save you some expense, and hope that you will practice extreme moderation when using these three recipes for a *Mud Pie*, *Buttery Nipple*, and a *B-52*, as well as any others you may uncover. Shooter drinks can be very rich and should never be consumed in excess.

Directions

Mud Pie:

1/4 vodka

1/4 vanilla liqueur

1/4 Bailey's Irish Cream

1/4 Kahlua coffee liqueur

Mix all four ingredients equally and pour into shot glass. Mud Pie is usually drank in one swallow.

A

Buttery Nipple:

1 oz. Buttershots liqueur (butterscotch flavor)

0.5 oz. Bailey's Irish Cream

Mix exact amount desired for number of shots at this ratio, in a shaker and shake gently for about 5 seconds, or until foam head develops. Pour into shot glasses and serve. A Buttery Nipple can be drank in one swallow, or sipped as a drink.

B

B-52:

1/3 Kahlua coffee liqueur

1/3 Amaretto almond liqueur

1/3 Bailey's Irish Cream

In a shaker mix exact amount desired for number of shots, at this ratio, and shake gently for about 5 seconds, or until foam head develops. Pour into shot glasses and serve. The B-52 is usually drank in one swallow.

C

Let us nay forget, that the reason Old Saint Nick is so jolly, is because he knows where all the bad girls live.

Hallucinations

Susie's Sippers

Ingredients

Liquor, More Liquor, then a little more liquor, and maybe some ice.

Description of these drinks is probably not necessary, so let me use this space to promote sensible and safe consumption. Drinks in the Hallucinations category, consist mainly of liquor, and are very strong. They will impair your ability to drive, operate equipment, or quite simply think. Be smart!

A Bone from Pennie

Can you still here those voices in your head KNUCKLEHEAD? Listen to the one that is repeating the words DANGER and THINK.

Hillbilly Eggnog is a sweet and refreshing drink, great for the summertime. The large amount of liquor is masked in this drink so sip slowly and do not have more than two of these if you plan on standing or walking. Forget about driving.

This twisted version of the Salty Dog has made the *Hairless Chihuahua* a popular drink with the college crowd. It is a pleasingly tasty drink that has been known to creep up on the unsuspecting.

LSD is the short name for *Lucifer In The Sky With Diamonds*, and rightfully so. This is a very powerful drink that glows in the dark under UV lights; Need I say more? Any whiskey can be used, and Southern Comfort is a common substitute for the Jack Daniels. Garnish with orange slice and fresh blueberries.

Directions

Hillbilly Eggnog:

1 oz. sweet vermouth

1 oz. gin

1 oz. cherry brandy

1 oz. orange juice

Place ingredients in shaker with ice and shake well for 10 seconds. Strain and serve in martini glass and garnish with orange slice and cherry.

Hairless Chihuahua

2 oz. tequila

1 oz. peach schnapps

3 oz. grapefruit juice (red or yellow)

Mix ingredients in a shaker with ice and shake vigorously for 5 seconds. Pour contents with ice into a large cocktail glass and garnish with cherry, and a mango or peach slice. Add dash of salt.

Lucifer In The Sky With Diamonds:

1.5 oz. Jack Daniels whiskey

1.5 oz. peach schnapps

4 oz. orange juice

0.5 ounce blue curacao liqueur

Mix whiskey, schnapps, and orange juice in a shaker with ice, and strain neat in cocktail glass. Drizzle blue curacao liqueur on top and serve.

A

B

C

Don't sweat the petty things, don't pet the sweaty things, and never drink alone when a good friend is nearby.

I thought it necessary to formally say good bye to all my new friends who have either purchased this book, or have received it as a gift. My writing experience up until this book consisted of one screen-play, so this book was not only a learning experience for me, but a giant wake up call as to the difficulty of this field of endeavor. Writers and photographers have my new earned respect.

The work was a labor of love, that proved so much more difficult than I had originally imagined, but it also proved to be as rewarding as I ever anticipated.

I send a special thanks out to my beloved mother, Jewell Pearman, living in Mountain Grove, Missouri, where cooking is still considered an art and a skill to share with both family and friends; not just when it is needed, but whenever you feel like being nice. I watched her work so hard, cooking at the public schools in Mountain Grove my entire childhood, and yet she always found time to let me help her cook on weekends, whenever I felt like it, and begin the process of learning how to cook. I love you Mom.

The last page contains my favorite quote of all time by Theodore Roosevelt. When not cooking, open the book to this quote, place it on a stand, and use it as decoration, and a daily reminder to always endeavor for success, without letting the fear of failure negatively effect your preparation or effort.

Now for all the rest of you **KNUCKLEHEADS**, *let me just say that if I have the pleasure of helping just one of you begin to enjoy the fun of cooking as much as I have, then I shall consider this book and writing endeavor to have been a total success. Enjoy the recipes, share them with family and friends, watch that waistline, and thank you for having such a good sense of humor.*

Bon appétit!

Happy Cooking KNUCKLeHeadS

Good Luck to all of my new friends; enjoy your new skills and my recipes.

The author, Harold W. Pearman, with his beautiful cooking tips corroborator, Pennie, at The Garden of the Gods in Colorado Springs, Colorado, where he resides, rides, relaxes, and cooks.

It is not the critic who counts; not the man who points out how the strong man stumbles, or where the doer of deeds could have done them better.

The credit belongs to the man who is actually in the arena, whose face is marred by dust and sweat and blood; who strives valiantly; who errs, who comes short again and again, because there is no effort without error and shortcoming; but who does actually strive to do the deeds; who knows great enthusiasms, the great devotions; who spends himself in a worthy cause; who at the best knows in the end the triumph of high achievement, and who at the worst, if he fails, at least fails while daring greatly, so that his place shall never be with those cold and timid souls who neither know victory nor defeat.

Theodore Roosevelt

CPSIA information can be obtained
at www.ICGtesting.com
Printed in the USA
LVXC01n1932151213
365414LV00024B/340